Endorsements for the Flourish Bible Study Series

"The brilliant and beautiful mix of sound teaching, helpful charts, lists, sidebars, and appealing graphics—as well as insightful questions that get the reader into the text of Scripture—make these studies that women will want to invest time in and will look back on as time well spent."
    Nancy Guthrie, Bible teacher; author, *Even Better than Eden*

"If you're looking for rich, accessible, and deeply biblical Bible studies, this series is for you! Lydia Brownback leads her readers through different books of the Bible, providing background information, maps, timelines, and questions that probe the text in order to glean understanding and application. She settles us deeply in the context of a book as she highlights God's unfolding plan of redemption and rescue. You will learn, you will delight in God's word, and you will love our good King Jesus even more."
    Courtney Doctor, Coordinator of Women's Initiatives, The Gospel Coalition; author, *From Garden to Glory* and *Steadfast*

"My daughter and I love using Flourish Bible Studies for our morning devotions. Lydia Brownback's faithful probing of biblical texts; insightful questions; invitations to engage in personal applications using additional biblical texts and historical contexts; and commitment to upholding the whole counsel of God as it bears on living life as a godly woman have drawn us closer to the Lord and to his word. Brownback never sidesteps hard questions or hard providences, but neither does she appeal to discourses of victimhood or therapy, which are painfully common in the genre of women's Bible studies. I cannot recommend this series highly enough. My daughter and I look forward to working through this whole series together!"
    Rosaria Butterfield, Former Professor of English, Syracuse University; author, *The Gospel Comes with a House Key*

"Lydia Brownback's Flourish Bible Study series has been a huge gift to the women's ministry in my local church. Many of our groups have gone through her studies in both the Old and New Testaments and have benefited greatly. The Flourish Bible Study series is now my go-to for a combination of rich Bible study, meaningful personal application, and practical group interaction. I recommend them whenever a partner in ministry asks me for quality women's Bible study resources. I'm so thankful Brownback continues to write them and share them with us!"
    Jen Oshman, author, *Enough about Me* and *Cultural Counterfeits*; Women's Ministry Director, Redemption Parker, Colorado

"Lydia Brownback has a contagious love for the Bible. Not only is she fluent in the best of biblical scholarship in the last generation, but her writing is accessible to the simplest of readers. She has the rare ability of being clear without being reductionistic. I anticipate many women indeed will flourish through her trustworthy guidance in this series."
    David Mathis, Senior Teacher and Executive Editor, desiringGod.org; Pastor, Cities Church, Saint Paul, Minnesota; author, *Habits of Grace*

"As a women's ministry leader, I am excited about the development of the Flourish Bible Study series, which will not only prayerfully equip women to increase in biblical literacy but also come alongside them to build a systematic and comprehensive framework to become lifelong students of the word of God. This series provides visually engaging studies with accessible content that will not only strengthen the believer but the church as well."
    Karen Hodge, Coordinator of Women's Ministries, Presbyterian Church in America; coauthor, *Transformed*

"Lydia Brownback is an experienced Bible teacher who has dedicated her life to ministry roles that help women (and men) grow in Christ. With a wealth of biblical, historical, and theological content, her Flourish Bible Studies are ideal for groups and individuals that are serious about the in-depth study of the word of God."
    Phil and Lisa Ryken, President, Wheaton College; and his wife, Lisa

"Lydia Brownback's Bible study series provides a faithful guide to book after book. You'll find rich insights into context and good questions to help you study and interpret the Bible. Page by page, the studies point you to respond to each passage and to love our great and gracious God. I will recommend the Flourish series for years to come for those looking for a wise, Christ-centered study that leads toward the goal of being transformed by the word."
    Taylor Turkington, Bible teacher; Director, BibleEquipping.org

ROMANS

Flourish Bible Study Series
By Lydia Brownback

Judges: The Path from Chaos to Kingship

Esther: The Hidden Hand of God

Job: Trusting God When Suffering Comes

Ecclesiastes: Finding Meaning When Life Feels Meaningless

Jonah: God's Relentless Grace

Habakkuk: Learning to Live by Faith

Luke: Good News of Great Joy

Romans: The Glory of the Gospel

Ephesians: Growing in Christ

Philippians: Living for Christ

Colossians: Fullness of Life in Christ

James: Walking in Wisdom

1–2 Peter: Living Hope in a Hard World

FLOURISH BIBLE STUDY

ROMANS

THE GLORY OF THE GOSPEL

LYDIA BROWNBACK

WHEATON, ILLINOIS

Romans: The Glory of the Gospel

© 2025 by Lydia Brownback

Published by Crossway
          1300 Crescent Street
          Wheaton, Illinois 60187

All rights reserved. No part of this publication may be reproduced, stored in a retrieval system, or transmitted in any form by any means, electronic, mechanical, photocopy, recording, or otherwise, without the prior permission of the publisher, except as provided for by USA copyright law. Crossway® is a registered trademark in the United States of America.

Cover design: Crystal Courtney

First printing 2025

Printed in China

Scripture quotations are from the ESV® Bible (The Holy Bible, English Standard Version®), © 2001 by Crossway, a publishing ministry of Good News Publishers. Used by permission. All rights reserved. The ESV text may not be quoted in any publication made available to the public by a Creative Commons license. The ESV may not be translated in whole or in part into any other language.

All emphases in Scripture quotations have been added by the author.

Trade paperback ISBN: 978-1-4335-9030-6

Crossway is a publishing ministry of Good News Publishers.

RRDS		34	33	32	31	30	29	28	27	26	25
15	14	13	12	11	10	9	8	7	6	5	4	3	2	1

With gratitude to God
for James Montgomery Boice (1938–2000),

who shepherded my faith
and set Romans in my soul.

"From him and through him and to him are all things.
To him be glory forever. Amen." —Romans 11:36

CONTENTS

The Timing of Romans x

Introduction: Getting into Romans xiii

Reading Plan xvii

Week 1   Righteousness Revealed (Romans 1:1–17) 1

Week 2   Rock Bottom (Romans 1:18–3:20) 11

Week 3   By Faith from Beginning to End (Romans 3:21–4:25) 25

Week 4   A Brand-New Reality (Romans 5:1–21) 35

Week 5   Set Free! (Romans 6:1–7:25) 45

Week 6   Your Best Life Now—and Always (Romans 8:1–39) 57

Week 7   All Hearts in God's Hands (Romans 9:1–33) 71

Week 8   Mystery Made Known (Romans 10:1–11:36) 81

Week 9   Be What You Are (Romans 12:1–15:13) 95

Week 10   A Portrait of Faithfulness (Romans 15:14–16:27) 109

Helpful Resources for Studying Romans 119

Notes 121

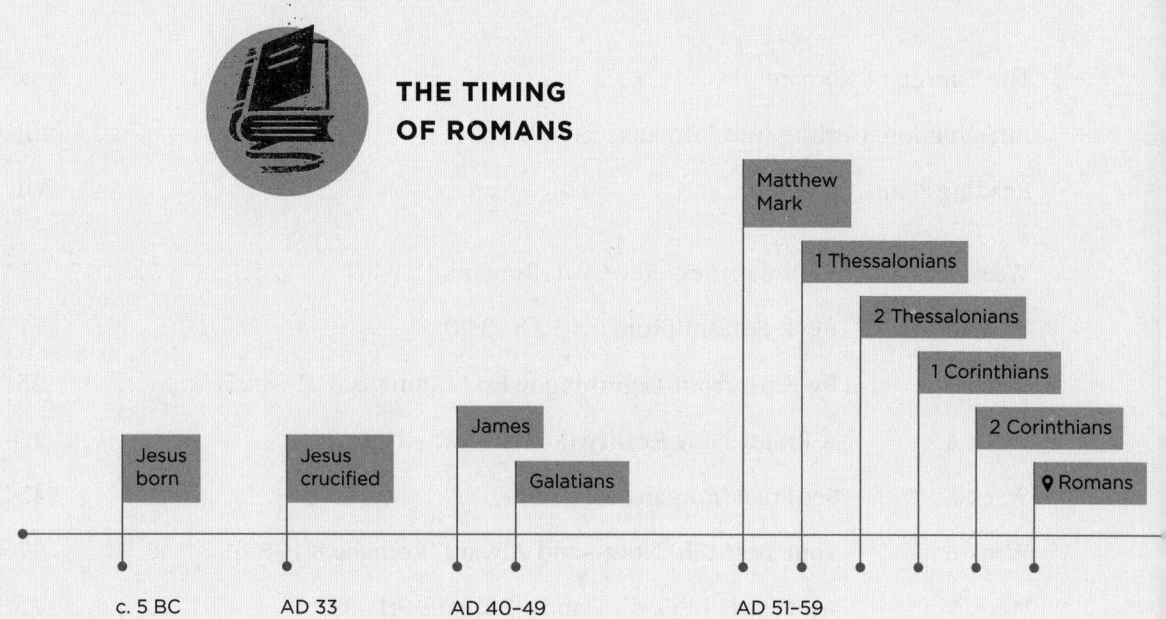

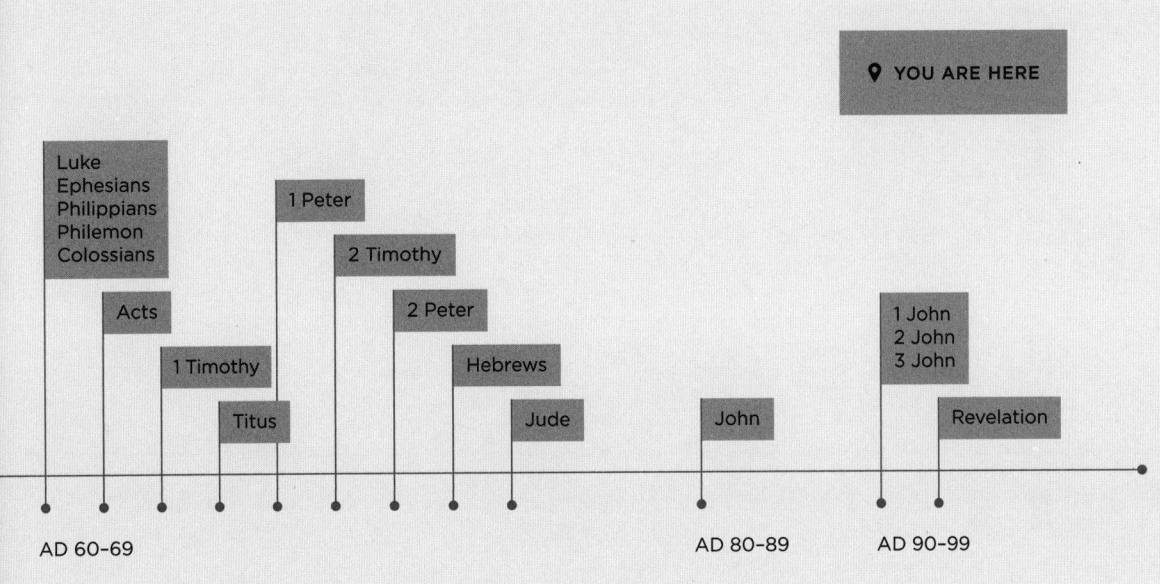

INTRODUCTION

GETTING INTO ROMANS

What is the gospel—the biblical gospel? I wonder if you get nervous when someone asks you to explain it. Those with a good grasp of Bible doctrine often have an answer ready at hand. Others feel some degree of confidence but suspect that if they're pushed for a detailed explanation, they might falter a bit. A good many dread being asked because they have very little confidence that they could provide a biblically faithful answer. If you want to grow your understanding of God's gospel, Romans is *the* Bible book for you. Here we learn all about how Jesus's death on the cross satisfied God's justice and opened the floodgates of his mercy.

WHO'S WHO IN ROMANS

The apostle Paul wrote this letter to Christians in the church (or churches) in Rome. Most likely, Paul wrote the letter while he was in the city of Corinth spreading the gospel message. He had never been to Rome, and he greatly desired to travel there to meet the Roman Christians in person. Those Christians in Rome were the recipients of Paul's letter. The Roman church was made up of both Jewish and non-Jewish (Gentile) believers. We get hints throughout the letter that the huge differences in the religious backgrounds of Jews and Gentiles were causing some tension and perhaps misunderstandings about the way God saves people. Romans 16 identifies several members of the Roman church by name, but we know very little about the majority of them beyond this. Important Old Testament figures are also found in Romans, including the very first man, Adam; the patriarch Abraham and his wife Sarah; and the prophet Elijah. Most important in Romans—the one who the letter is all about—is God in three persons: God the Father, Jesus Christ the Son, and the Holy Spirit.

SETTING

The church in Rome was quite well established when Paul wrote his letter. We learn in Acts 2:10–11 that "visitors from Rome" were present at Pentecost, when the Holy Spirit descended on believers in power. After this pivotal event, it's likely that those Roman visitors returned to their hometown and began to build the church there in Rome. At its beginning, the church was made up mostly of believing Jews, but in time, pressures from the government forced the Jews out of the city. During their absence, the church experienced an influx of Gentile converts. Later, the Jews filtered back into Rome, and at the time of Paul's letter, they were once again participating in church life with the Gentile believers.

Rome in the Time of Paul (c. AD 60)[1]

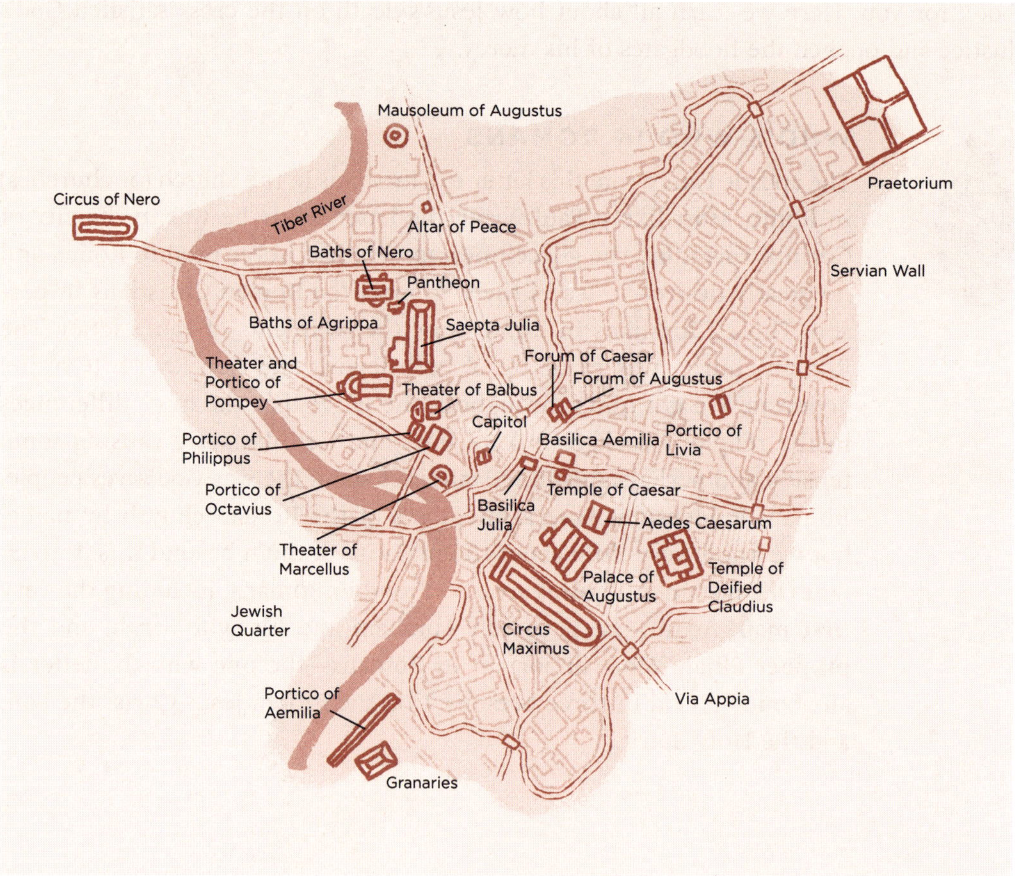

THEMES

Paul is eager to show the believers in Rome that people from every tribe, nation, and ethnicity have always been a part of God's plan for salvation. As Paul addresses this issue, we learn a great deal about God's sovereign power to save, how he works in hearts to accomplish salvation, and what is required to receive it. In all this, the great doctrines of the faith are unfolded for us, and as we study them, we'll realize why these doctrines aren't just for ivory-tower theologians. They have very practical implications for our day-to-day lives.

STUDYING ROMANS

At the beginning of each week's lesson, read the entire passage. And then read it again. If you are studying Romans with a group, read it once more, aloud, when you gather to discuss the lesson. *Marinating in the Scripture text is the most important part of any Bible study.*

> "This book is the place where the gospel of Christ shines most brightly and most thoroughly in all the Bible"[2]

GROUP STUDY

If you are doing this study as part of a group, you'll want to finish each week's lesson before the group meeting. As you prepare, you can work your way through the study questions all in one sitting or by doing a little bit each day. And don't be discouraged if you don't have sufficient time to answer every question. Just do as much as you can, knowing that the more you do, the more you'll learn. No matter how much of the study you are able to complete each week, the group will benefit simply from your presence, so don't skip the gathering if you can't finish! That being said, group time will be most rewarding for every participant if you have done the lesson in advance. When you gather, read the entire passage aloud either before your discussion or a bit at a time as you make your way through the material. Feel free to structure group time in whatever way seems best for your particular setup. You can move through the study questions and answers together, addressing all or some of them, or you can stay anchored on the Bible passage itself, using the questions and answers as more of a discussion tool as needed.

If you are leading the group, you can scan or visit crossway.org/Romans LeadersGuide to download a free leader's guide with study tips and answers to discussion questions.

INDIVIDUAL STUDY

The study is designed to run for ten weeks, but you can set your own pace if you're studying solo. And you can download the free leader's guide (crossway.org/RomansLeadersGuide) if you'd like some guidance along the way.

Marinating in the Scripture text is the most important part of any Bible study.

Reading Plan

	Primary Text	Supplemental Reading
Week 1	Romans 1:1–17	Genesis 12:1–4; Habakkuk 2:4
Week 2	Romans 1:18–3:20	
Week 3	Romans 3:21–4:25	Genesis 15:1–6; Psalm 32
Week 4	Romans 5:1–21	Genesis 3:1–19
Week 5	Romans 6:1–7:25	
Week 6	Romans 8:1–39	Galatians 5:16–26
Week 7	Romans 9:1–33	
Week 8	Romans 10:1–11:36	
Week 9	Romans 12:1–15:13	
Week 10	Romans 15:14–16:27	Genesis 3:14–15

WEEK 1

RIGHTEOUSNESS REVEALED

ROMANS 1:1-17

The most hope-filled word of all time is *gospel*, and for good reason: it means "good news." Maybe that's why this beautiful word permeates Christian lingo. There are *gospel* conversations and *gospel-driven* ministries, and particular situations marked as *gospel* issues. But there's a danger in using this lovely word in such varied ways. Over time, these varied uses of the word *gospel* risk obscuring its true, biblical meaning. The gospel of the Bible is about one specific thing—salvation in Christ Jesus for sinners. *This* is the gospel that the apostle Paul was so passionate to share far and wide. His passion is evident from the very beginning of the letter. In these opening verses we discover a lot about the apostle's heart, not only for God's gospel, but for people and, more than anything else, for the Lord Jesus Christ. Paul's heart is evident in his greetings—the longest of any in his letters—and in his desire to come to Rome and visit these fellow believers face-to-face. He rejoices in all God has done through the gospel to save sinners, and as we study his words, we can't help but find ourselves rejoicing along with him. His passion for the gospel is contagious!

> *"The gospel is not a break with the past, rather it is the continuation and consummation of it."*[3]

1. SET APART (1:1–7)

Paul's lengthy opening is no ordinary introduction! Not only do we meet this great apostle, but we also get our first glimpse of his overarching message—the gospel.

> ¹Paul, a servant of Christ Jesus, called to be an apostle, set apart for the gospel of God … (v. 1)

✦ What three things do we learn about Paul in verse 1?

1. _____
2. _____
3. _____

With credentials like these, all he's about to share can surely be trusted. First, he wants his readers to know that he's completely sold out to the Lord and lives to serve him. He has no other agenda. Added to this is his authoritative role, one given to him by Jesus Christ himself (you can read about it in Acts 9:1–19). Paul and the other men in this role, the apostles, were directly called by Christ to lead the early church. This call on Paul's life was the foundation for his overarching mission, what he's been set apart to do—make the gospel known.

As all good preachers do, Paul quickly changes the subject from himself to the gospel of God:

> … ²which he promised beforehand through his prophets in the holy Scriptures, ³concerning his Son, who was descended from David according to the flesh ⁴and was declared to be the Son of God in power according to the Spirit of holiness by his resurrection from the dead, Jesus Christ our Lord, ⁵through whom we have received grace and apostleship to bring about the obedience of faith for the sake of his name among all the nations, ⁶including you who are called to belong to Jesus Christ." (vv. 2–6)

The first thing we learn about the gospel is that it's not confined to the New Testament. This good news (remember that the word *gospel* actually means "good news") was foretold by the Old Testament prophets.

Paul's overarching point about the gospel is that it's all about God's Son, Jesus Christ. The name Jesus means "God saves." *Christ* isn't his last name—it's his title. It's the same as the Old Testament term *messiah*, which means "anointed one."

Although Jesus Christ is God's Son, he's not inferior to God the Father. He is equal in power and being and might and has always existed. At the appointed time, the Son of God was born into the world, taking on a human nature without ever losing his divine nature. The Old Testament promises make clear that this Savior-Son would descend from the royal line of Israel's King David, and that's exactly what happened. After Jesus died on the cross, he was raised from the dead, which marked the beginning of his glorious reign as the God-man for all eternity. That's the "power" Paul has in mind here in verse 4.

- It is through the resurrected Lord Jesus that grace comes to believers and transforms their lives, what Paul calls "the obedience of faith" in verse 5. What does Paul say here is the ultimate reason for why we receive this grace?

Paul concludes his lengthy introduction by addressing the Roman Christians directly:

> ⁷ To all those in Rome who are loved by God and called to be saints: Grace to you and peace from God our Father and the Lord Jesus Christ. (v. 7)

- The Roman Christians (and all Christians in every age) are marked out as "saints." Our identity as a saint doesn't mean we have to worry about presenting a flawless self to the world around us. Paul isn't lecturing us to be do-gooders to earn God's favor. *Saints* in the New Testament means "set apart" or "different." In light of everything Paul has said in these opening verses, what is it that makes a Christian set apart or different?

> *"Grace is getting what we do not deserve from God, namely, His pardon, peace, joy, and deliverance from His wrath for our sins against him."*[4]

2. THE PASSION OF PAUL'S HEART (1:8–15)

Paul has longed to visit the Christians in Rome and carry on his gospel ministry in this hub of the world, and he begins with gratitude that the gospel is reaching not only God's Jewish people but also Gentiles, the Bible's term for people outside the nation of Israel:

> [8] First, I thank my God through Jesus Christ for all of you, because your faith is proclaimed in all the world. [9] For God is my witness, whom I serve with my spirit in the gospel of his Son, that without ceasing I mention you [10] always in my prayers, asking that somehow by God's will I may now at last succeed in coming to you. [11] For I long to see you, that I may impart to you some spiritual gift to strengthen you— [12] that is, that we may be mutually encouraged by each other's faith, both yours and mine. (vv. 8–12)

✦ What do we learn about the blessings of in-person fellowship from Paul's desire to visit Rome?

_____
_____
_____
_____

Paul expresses again his longtime desire to visit:

> [13] I do not want you to be unaware, brothers, that I have often intended to come to you (but thus far have been prevented), in order that I may reap some harvest among you as well as among the rest of the Gentiles. [14] I am under obligation both to Greeks and to barbarians, both to the wise and to the foolish. [15] So I am eager to preach the gospel to you also who are in Rome. (vv. 13–15)

✦ Given all he's said so far, how would you define the "harvest" Paul hopes to reap in Rome?

✦ Why do you think Paul says he is "under obligation" to preach the gospel?

We might think of a barbarian (v.14) as a rough-and-tumble person who lives against the grain of polite society, but that's not how Paul uses the word. The barbarians were people outside of the typical Greek culture of his day. Paul contrasts barbarians to people immersed in Greek society and who spoke the Greek language. He's saying that the gospel is not restricted to a particular ethnic group or socioeconomic class—it's for everyone.

Paul plans to "reap a harvest" among the recipients of his letter—the saints in Rome. Why would he include believers, who already know the gospel? His intentions here reveal an important truth: the gospel isn't only for the lost; it's for the already saved too. It's the instrument that brings the lost to Christ, but it's also the means through which believers continue with Christ and grow up in their faith. Even as we grow in our Christian life, we never outgrow the gospel.

3. WHAT IT'S ALL ABOUT (1:16–17)

Paul wraps up his introduction and transitions into the heart of his message by setting out his overarching theme, not only of the letter but of his entire life—the gospel:

> ¹⁶ For I am not ashamed of the gospel, for it is the power of God for salvation to everyone who believes, to the Jew first and also to the Greek. ¹⁷ For in it

the righteousness of God is revealed from faith for faith, as it is written, "The righteous shall live by faith." (vv. 16–17)

- He builds his case for the gospel, using the word *for*, or "for this reason," four times in these two verses. Look at how these *fors* follow one from another, and then answer the following questions:

  · Why is Paul not ashamed of the gospel?

  · Why is the gospel God's power for salvation?

  · What does the gospel bring to light?

  · How is the gospel received?

How do you react when someone mocks God's words and ways or when people look down on you for believing that Jesus lived and died for your salvation? If you hide your beliefs or change your convictions under such pressure, you know what it means to be "ashamed" of the gospel (v. 16). Paul wasn't ashamed, even when his beliefs proved life-threatening, and he explains why in these verses. A righteous God declares unrighteous people "righteous" when they forsake faith in themselves and rest all their faith in the perfect righteousness of the God-man Jesus Christ.

✦ Why do you think people might ever feel ashamed of this gospel?

A bit of explanation for some of Paul's wording in these verses might be helpful.

First, although Paul seems to prioritize the Jews for salvation, his words are about *chronology*, not *priority*. The Jews (Israel) were set apart in the Old Testament for special blessings, but God's intention was always to enfold people from every race and ethnicity to share in these blessings. All the way back in Genesis, from the very first book of the Bible, this is made clear (take a look at Genesis 12:1–4).

Second, when Paul says that God's righteousness is revealed "from faith for faith," it's his way of saying that salvation is rooted in faith from beginning to end.

Third, Paul quotes the Old Testament prophet Habakkuk, "The righteous shall live by faith." Habakkuk prophesied during a very grim time in the history of God's people, a time when God's righteous anger against sin resulted in painful suffering. But all that suffering was designed to fuel their faith and restore their wayward hearts to God. In every age, what saves people from God's righteous wrath is faith in God and his promises.

> *"Paul was in love with Jesus Christ, and it was his love for Christ that alone explains the nature and rigor of his life's work."*[5]

LET'S TALK

1. If you are a Christian, then you are a saint. Discuss what this means practically. In other words, how can knowing that this is your identity shape—or reshape—the way you live?

2. Talk about situations in which you find yourself "ashamed" or embarrassed to be aligned with the gospel. What do you think underlies your embarrassment? From all Paul wrote in his introduction, what most helps you fight that temptation?

3. The apostle Paul was motivated by love for the gospel, for people, and primarily for Jesus Christ. In what ways does your love for Jesus reflect Paul's, and in what ways does it fall short? Our love for Christ grows as we realize the depth of our sinfulness. Discuss why this is true.

WEEK 2

ROCK BOTTOM

ROMANS 1:18–3:20

The good news of the gospel is *rescue*. When we place our faith in the Lord Jesus Christ, we're rescued from sin and from ourselves, and our unrighteousness is covered by the perfect righteousness of Jesus Christ. We can know these gospel facts and believe them, but only a realistic look at the terrible, horrible awfulness of sin enables us to get why the gospel is such very good news. We need to see what exactly we've been rescued *from* in order to rejoice in what we've been rescued *to*. A closer look at this portion of Romans is exactly what we need. Here we see just how sinful sin truly is—including our very own sin. That's what Paul shows us this week. Glimpsing this awfulness gives us a better understanding of God's righteousness, which is something we're given in the gospel. And as we see the horror of sin, the way it poisons us in mind, body, and soul, God's wrath begins to make absolute sense. After diving deep into these early chapters of Romans, we can't help but come away with brand-new wonder and awe about what God has done for us in Christ.

> *"Man as sinner hates God, hates man, and hates himself. He would kill God if he could. He does kill his fellow man when he can. And he commits spiritual suicide every day of his life."*[6]

1. NO EXCUSE! (1:18–32)

No sooner has Paul encouraged us with the good news of the gospel than he seems to unnerve us with God's wrath. But the truth is, we can't really grasp why the gospel is such good news if we don't understand God's wrath and the reason for it. Paul makes it abundantly clear as he describes human beings in their natural, unsaved state:

> [18] For the wrath of God is revealed from heaven against all ungodliness and unrighteousness of men, who by their unrighteousness suppress the truth. [19] For what can be known about God is plain to them, because God has shown it to them. [20] For his invisible attributes, namely, his eternal power and divine nature, have been clearly perceived, ever since the creation of the world, in the things that have been made. So they are without excuse. [21] For although they knew God, they did not honor him as God or give thanks to him, but they became futile in their thinking, and their foolish hearts were darkened. [22] Claiming to be wise, they became fools, [23] and exchanged the glory of the immortal God for images resembling mortal man and birds and animals and creeping things. (1:18–23)

✦ What particular act of unrighteousness does Paul identify in verse 18?

✦ From this passage, what can be known about God from created things?

✦ Why do human beings have no excuse for this unrighteousness?

Romans 1:18–3:20

✝ What sins does Paul name in verse 21, and what happens to the minds and hearts of those who commit these sins?

> **Idolatry**
>
> "Idolatry is the fundamental sin.... In addition to the images housed in great temples, Roman families commonly kept representations of individual 'house gods' in their homes.... Modern 'idols' don't look like ancient ones; images served today are often mental rather than metal. But people still devote their lives to, and trust in, many things other than God."[7]

How ironic that those who reject God believe they are wise for doing so! The reality is, they are fools because they devote themselves to God's creation rather than to God himself. The primary sin in view here is idolatry.

Judgment for these sins—the outworking of God's wrath—is described in all its horror:

> ²⁴ Therefore God gave them up in the lusts of their hearts to impurity, to the dishonoring of their bodies among themselves, ²⁵ because they exchanged the truth about God for a lie and worshiped and served the creature rather than the Creator, who is blessed forever! Amen. ²⁶ For this reason God gave them up to dishonorable passions. For their women exchanged natural relations for those that are contrary to nature; ²⁷ and the men likewise gave up natural relations with women and were consumed with passion for one another, men committing shameless acts with men and receiving in themselves the due penalty for

their error. ²⁸ And since they did not see fit to acknowledge God, God gave them up to a debased mind to do what ought not to be done. ²⁹ They were filled with all manner of unrighteousness, evil, covetousness, malice. They are full of envy, murder, strife, deceit, maliciousness. They are gossips, ³⁰ slanderers, haters of God, insolent, haughty, boastful, inventors of evil, disobedient to parents, ³¹ foolish, faithless, heartless, ruthless. ³² Though they know God's righteous decree that those who practice such things deserve to die, they not only do them but give approval to those who practice them. (1:24–32)

Unrepentant sinners may joke about the wrathful strike of divine lightning, but God typically judges unrepentant sin, not by lightning strikes, but by the sin itself. In other words, to those who persistently reject God and seek to replace him with things in creation, God will eventually say to them, "Have it your way." It's what Paul means by "God gave them up."

✚ Identify each instance of "God gave them up" in this passage. What is it that people are given up *to*, and in each case, how does this *giving up* work out in their lives?

- 1:24–25

- 1:26–27

- 1:28–32

2. SELF-DECEIVED (2:1–16)

Where the last section, 1:18–32, was describing unsaved Gentiles, Paul now turns his attention to God's people Israel, the Jews, who might be reading all Paul has just written and thinking, *Whew! That lets me off the hook because I'm not like those wicked people.* But not so fast:

> ¹Therefore you have no excuse, O man, every one of you who judges. For in passing judgment on another you condemn yourself, because you, the judge, practice the very same things. ²We know that the judgment of God rightly falls on those who practice such things. ³Do you suppose, O man—you who judge those who practice such things and yet do them yourself—that you will escape the judgment of God? ⁴Or do you presume on the riches of his kindness and forbearance and patience, not knowing that God's kindness is meant to lead you to repentance? ⁵But because of your hard and impenitent heart you are storing up wrath for yourself on the day of wrath when God's righteous judgment will be revealed. (2:1–5)

✦ In 1:20 Paul declares that human beings are "without excuse." He makes the same accusation here in 2:1. What reason is given in each case?

- 1:20

- 2:1

> "We are at war with God. In effect, we hate him; at the very least we do not want him to rule over our lives and resent any meaningful attempts he makes to do so. Romans shows how God deals with this problem."[8]

✦ Those who point a judgmental finger at others are hypocrites because they "practice the very same things" (2:1). What "same things" does Paul have in mind here?

> ### Imputation
>
> The word *imputation* is an accounting term; it means "to apply to one's account." Our sin was imputed to Christ—Christ took our sin on himself. Our great debit was put on his account. And Christ's righteousness is imputed to us. He not only takes our debit, but we also get His credit.[9]

✦ Paul asks these hypocrites a rhetorical question: Do you suppose . . . that you will escape the judgment of God?" (2:3). That's indeed exactly what many of the Jews thought. Because for centuries they'd been God's special, chosen people, they presumed they were safe from judgment. Oh, how wrong they were! For what will they be judged?

✦ Knowing the true God changes us. How is that shown in verse 4?

God isn't unfair. That's the point Paul is making, and he works this out next:

> ⁶ He will render to each one according to his works: ⁷ to those who by patience in well-doing seek for glory and honor and immortality, he will give eternal life; ⁸ but for those who are self-seeking and do not obey the truth, but obey unrighteousness, there will be wrath and fury. ⁹ There will be tribulation and distress for every human being who does evil, the Jew first and also the Greek, ¹⁰ but glory and honor and peace for everyone who does good, the Jew first and also the Greek. ¹¹ For God shows no partiality. (2:6–11)

✚ Every one of us—Jew and Gentile alike—will be judged by God for what we do. How are the righteous contrasted with the unrighteous in verses 6–11?

The Righteous	The Unrighteous

Paul elaborates on why God's judgment is just:

> ¹²For all who have sinned without the law will also perish without the law, and all who have sinned under the law will be judged by the law. ¹³For it is not the hearers of the law who are righteous before God, but the doers of the law who will be justified. ¹⁴For when Gentiles, who do not have the law, by nature do what the law requires, they are a law to themselves, even though they do not have the law. ¹⁵They show that the work of the law is written on their hearts, while their conscience also bears witness, and their conflicting thoughts accuse or even excuse them ¹⁶on that day when, according to my gospel, God judges the secrets of men by Christ Jesus. (2:12–16)

The Jews thought they had salvation all figured out because, historically, they'd been the ones to whom God revealed his ways and gave his law through Moses in the Old Testament, what theologians call the "Mosaic law" or the "old covenant." But, Paul says, knowing the law won't do them any good in the long run because, as he's been making clear, they've failed to obey it. And certainly the Gentiles who've never been taught the law can't obey what they don't even know. Yet, as Paul clarifies, even if they were never taught God's law, it's written on their hearts. So they *do* know, which is clear from the fact that their conscience bothers them when they break it. Whether Jews who were given God's law or Gentiles who lacked that earlier advantage, the overarching point in these verses is this: "*having* the law is not what matters—*obeying* it is."[10]

As for the Jews, they can't lean on learning and tradition for salvation:

> ¹⁷But if you call yourself a Jew and rely on the law and boast in God ¹⁸and know his will and approve what is excellent, because you are instructed from the law; ¹⁹and if you are sure that you yourself are a guide to the blind, a light to those who are in darkness, ²⁰an instructor of the foolish, a teacher of children, having in the law the embodiment of knowledge and truth—²¹you then who teach others, do you not teach yourself? While you preach against stealing, do you steal? ²²You who say that one must not commit adultery, do you commit adultery? You who abhor idols, do you rob temples? ²³You who boast in the law dishonor God by breaking the law. ²⁴For, as it is written, "The name of God is blasphemed among the Gentiles because of you." (2:17–24)

✦ It's clear that the Jews thought that simply knowing the law was sufficient. How does Paul blow up this wrong thinking in verses 23–24?

3. WHAT COUNTS—AND WHAT DOESN'T (2:25–3:8)

Not only did the Jewish people possess God's law; they also practiced the rite of circumcision. All Jewish males were circumcised as a sign indicating their belonging with God's covenant people, and here Paul speaks directly about that old-covenant ritual:

> ²⁵ For circumcision indeed is of value if you obey the law, but if you break the law, your circumcision becomes uncircumcision. ²⁶ So, if a man who is uncircumcised keeps the precepts of the law, will not his uncircumcision be regarded as circumcision? ²⁷ Then he who is physically uncircumcised but keeps the law will condemn you who have the written code and circumcision but break the law. ²⁸ For no one is a Jew who is merely one outwardly, nor is circumcision outward and physical. ²⁹ But a Jew is one inwardly, and circumcision is a matter of the heart, by the Spirit, not by the letter. His praise is not from man but from God. (2:25–29)

From the way Paul explains the nature of this circumcision custom, it seems the Jews to whom he's writing viewed their circumcision as another kind of "spiritual security."[11]

✦ How does Paul debunk the Jews' wrong thinking in this passage?

"Jesus does not excuse us; he forgives us."[12]

✦ Why were the Gentiles *not* at a spiritual disadvantage by virtue of being uncircumcised?

Paul realizes that some of his Jewish readers might take issue about being on equal spiritual footing with the Gentiles,[13] so he conducts an imaginary dialogue with these objectors:

> ¹ Then what advantage has the Jew? Or what is the value of circumcision? ² Much in every way. To begin with, the Jews were entrusted with the oracles of God. ³ What if some were unfaithful? Does their faithlessness nullify the faithfulness of God? ⁴ By no means! Let God be true though every one were a liar, as it is written,
>
> > "That you may be justified in your words,
> >   and prevail when you are judged."
>
> ⁵ But if our unrighteousness serves to show the righteousness of God, what shall we say? That God is unrighteous to inflict wrath on us? (I speak in a human way.) ⁶ By no means! For then how could God judge the world? ⁷ But if through my lie God's truth abounds to his glory, why am I still being condemned as a sinner? ⁸ And why not do evil that good may come?—as some people slanderously charge us with saying. Their condemnation is just. (3:1–8)

The Jews had a lot of spiritual privileges. Generation after generation, God's promises had been taught and handed down from father to son. They knew they were God's special, set-apart people by covenant and basked in the security they believed it gave them, even when they'd been unfaithful to him. Yet through those dark times, God remained faithful to them, and, in fact, his grace shines brightest against the backdrop of their unfaithfulness. So, his opponents argue, if their sin makes God look good, why should they be held accountable for their sin? That's the gist of Paul's imaginary dialogue here. The overarching point in these verses is that unbelieving Jews dislike the gospel because it reveals that their Jewish privileges don't give them any spiritual advantages.

4. WHY WE NEED SALVATION (3:9–20)

Paul, drawing from his own Jewish background, cites some Old Testament passages to reinforce all he's been saying, which is that no one merits God's favor:

> ⁹ What then? Are we Jews any better off? No, not at all. For we have already charged that all, both Jews and Greeks, are under sin, ¹⁰ as it is written:
>
> "None is righteous, no, not one;
> ¹¹   no one understands;
>   no one seeks for God.
> ¹² All have turned aside; together they have become worthless;
>   no one does good,
>   not even one."
> ¹³ "Their throat is an open grave;
>   they use their tongues to deceive."
> "The venom of asps is under their lips."
> ¹⁴   "Their mouth is full of curses and bitterness."
> ¹⁵ "Their feet are swift to shed blood;
> ¹⁶   in their paths are ruin and misery,
> ¹⁷ and the way of peace they have not known."
> ¹⁸   "There is no fear of God before their eyes." (3:9–18)

✢ What more do these quotes, taken from the Psalms, reveal about the way human beings naturally relate to God? (Paul's quotes here come from Psalm 14:1–3; Psalm 5:9; and Psalm 10:7, in that order.)

Here is Paul's summary of all he's been saying to the recipients of his letter, both Jews and Gentiles:

> ¹⁹ Now we know that whatever the law says it speaks to those who are under the law, so that every mouth may be stopped, and the whole world may be held accountable to God. ²⁰ For by works of the law no human being will be justified in his sight, since through the law comes knowledge of sin. (3:19–20)

✝ We get insight in verses 19–20 about why God gave his law in the first place. First, it was given to reveal much about *God*—what a holy and just God requires of people. Second, it was given to reveal much about *human beings*. According to Paul's summary remarks here, what is this revelation?

LET'S TALK

1. Talk about the way God's judgment often plays out in his giving people over to their sin. How does that downward spiral progress? Where do you see indicators of this kind of judgment playing out in the world around you?

2. Crystal clear this week is that no one can merit God's favor, either by background or behavior. What spiritual privileges apart from Christ—or more likely, in addition to Christ—might you be tempted to rely on to earn God's favor? Consider things like theological knowledge, going to the "right" church, or being raised in a Christian home. Discuss what you learned in this week's lesson that debunks the idea of anything besides Christ as a means of righteousness.

3. Paul tells us in 2:7 that our good works matter: "To those who by patience in well-doing seek for glory and honor and immortality, he will give eternal life." We know now that our good works don't earn our salvation, but those works do prove whether or not Christ has saved us. Discuss why good works inevitably accompany salvation. You might want to take a look at James 2:14–17.

WEEK 3

BY FAITH FROM BEGINNING TO END

ROMANS 3:21–4:25

We've heard the bad news—nothing we do can make us right in God's eyes. Having faced this reality, we can receive the good news of the gospel with great joy because we see how much we need it. The heart of the gospel is found in the passage we're studying this week. Here we see that since we have no righteousness of our own, God provided it for us by sending his very own Son, Jesus Christ, to pay the penalty for our sins through his death on the cross. And the way we receive it is simply by faith. This isn't the first time Paul has told us this good news; in fact, he's been telling us the gospel truth from the beginning of the letter. His emphasis on the gospel just goes to show that we need to hear it again and again. The more we hear it, the more it grips us and shapes us. Paul is keen to reach the skeptics of his day, particularly the Jews who believed that their heritage as God's chosen people guaranteed their spiritual security. In this section of the letter, he employs a wise strategy for breaking through their hard hearts, showing that two of the greatest Israelites in history—the patriarch Abraham and the mighty King David—were both saved by faith and not by their greatness. We learn a lot this week about the nature of genuine faith, and we can examine our own hearts in light of what we learn.

1. A GRACIOUS GIFT (3:21–26)

Early in the letter, when Paul began to explain salvation, he told us that in the gospel, "the righteousness of God is revealed" (1:17). The righteousness he spoke of there is something God *gives*—the righteousness that comes through Christ. Here, having exposed us to why human beings are desperately in need of this righteousness, Paul circles back to it:

> [21] But now the righteousness of God has been manifested apart from the law, although the Law and the Prophets bear witness to it—[22] the righteousness of God through faith in Jesus Christ for all who believe. For there is no distinction: [23] for all have sinned and fall short of the glory of God, [24] and are justified by his grace as a gift, through the redemption that is in Christ Jesus, [25] whom God put forward as a propitiation by his blood, to be received by faith. This was to show God's righteousness, because in his divine forbearance he had passed over former sins. [26] It was to show his righteousness at the present time, so that he might be just and the justifier of the one who has faith in Jesus. (3:21–26)

The Old Testament prophets pointed forward in history to the coming of the righteous one, Jesus. God's law was meant to do the same thing. The law revealed that God's standards are so high and holy that no one can measure up. All through history, God was exposing man's dilemma and pointing ahead to the remedy for it.

Altogether, the entire Old Testament looked ahead to what Paul writes about here.

> *"The grace of God will never be withheld because of anything we may have done, however evil it was, nor will it be lessened because of that or any other evil we may do."*[14]

✚ To be "justified" by God is to be declared righteous in his eyes. According to 3:24, how does this justified status come to us? (Hint: take a look at the "Gospel Terms" chart on p. 27.)

Gospel Terms	
Justified	A legal term, a declaration of righteousness. Sinners are pardoned by God the judge. God placed our sin on Jesus, and placed Christ's righteousness on us. Now, clothed in the righteousness of Christ, we are accepted by God. A justified child of God can never be condemned.
Grace	God's undeserved favor to show kindness and favor to people who deserve the exact opposite—his wrath.
Redemption	In Bible times, slaves could be redeemed from enslavement through a payment—they were redeemed by money. In a similar way, we are redeemed from slavery to sin by the payment of a price—the blood of Christ on the cross.
Propitiation	Our sin was laid on Christ, and on the cross he died the death we deserve in order to satisfy or appease God's just wrath against our sin. Jesus himself was the *propitiation*, and God was the one *propitiated*.
Atonement	In order for our sin to be dealt with, a penalty must be paid. Jesus paid that penalty as our substitute. He took on himself what we deserve and in this way *atoned* for our sin.

✦ In 3:24, God's righteousness is something he *gives*, but in 3:25 it's what God *demands*. And because this is true, unrighteousness must be punished. God would be untrue to himself if he merely excused sin or swept it under the rug. It has to be paid for. According to verse 25, how was this payment made, and who initiated the payment? (If you need help, look again at the "Gospel Terms" chart.)

✣ Considering all we've uncovered in 3:21–26, explain why Paul says that God is both "just and the justifier of the one who has faith in Jesus" (v. 26).

2. FAITH ALONE (3:27-31)

So what does all this mean? There is only one fitting response to what Paul has just told us about salvation:

> ²⁷ Then what becomes of our boasting? It is excluded. By what kind of law? By a law of works? No, but by the law of faith. ²⁸ For we hold that one is justified by faith apart from works of the law. ²⁹ Or is God the God of Jews only? Is he not the God of Gentiles also? Yes, of Gentiles also, ³⁰ since God is one—who will justify the circumcised by faith and the uncircumcised through faith. ³¹ Do we then overthrow the law by this faith? By no means! On the contrary, we uphold the law. (3:27–31)

✣ Paul's words in verses 27–31 are meant to uncover attitudes of the heart. What heart posture do you think is necessary to embrace the truth that faith is the only grounds for salvation?

✦ In these verses Paul seeks to break down barriers between Jews and Gentiles and create unity between them. What does this convey to us about God's plan for his people, the church?

_____

_____

_____

_____

In this section Paul makes a crucial point, one he will make again, and in more detail, later in the letter. Here he frames it with a question: "Do we then overthrow the law by this faith? By no means! On the contrary, we uphold the law" (3:31). His point is, just because we are saved by faith doesn't mean obedience to God's law doesn't matter. To the contrary, the law is written on our hearts so that we desire to please God with our obedience. Paul is simply emphasizing the truth that obedience doesn't save us, but if we are truly saved, we will obey.

3. ALWAYS AND FOR EVERYONE (4:1–12)

Among the Jews of Paul's day, Abraham and David were two of the most well-regarded figures from Israel's history, which is likely why Paul brings them into the letter here, to drive home his point about salvation:

> ¹ What then shall we say was gained by Abraham, our forefather according to the flesh? ² For if Abraham was justified by works, he has something to boast about, but not before God. ³ For what does the Scripture say? "Abraham believed God, and it was counted to him as righteousness." ⁴ Now to the one who works, his wages are not counted as a gift but as his due. ⁵ And to the one who does not work but believes in him who justifies the ungodly, his faith is counted as righteousness, ⁶ just as David also speaks of the blessing of the one to whom God counts righteousness apart from works:
>
> ⁷ "Blessed are those whose lawless deeds are forgiven,
>   and whose sins are covered;
> ⁸ blessed is the man against whom the Lord will not count his sin." (4:1–8)

✦ Consider all the accounting terms Paul uses in Romans 4:1–8. He makes the point that workers are owed a paycheck: "To the one who works, his wages are not counted as a gift but as his due" (v. 4). According to Paul, how is God's economy radically different?

In 4:1–8, Paul looks back to an episode in Abraham's life, which is recorded for us in Genesis 15. The Lord appeared to childless Abraham in a vision and promised him a son and heir. Not only that, but the Lord promised that Abraham would have so many descendants that they'd be as numerous as stars in the sky. After hearing God's promise, Abraham "believed the Lord, and he counted it to him as righteousness" (Genesis 15:6).

Then Paul draws from Psalm 32, which King David wrote after experiencing God's forgiveness for his sin.

So, is the gift of faith only for Jewish people like Abraham, those who bore the mark of circumcision? That's the issue Paul has been dealing with, and the question he answers next:

> ⁹ Is this blessing then only for the circumcised, or also for the uncircumcised? For we say that faith was counted to Abraham as righteousness. ¹⁰ How then was it counted to him? Was it before or after he had been circumcised? It was not after, but before he was circumcised. (4:9–10)

✦ How does Abraham's story provide the answer to Paul's question in verse 9: "Is this blessing then only for the circumcised, or also for the uncircumcised?"

Paul's example of Abraham, the revered Jewish patriarch, had direct application for the Jews reading the letter. So, then, what about the Gentiles? Does Abraham's story have any application for them? That's what Paul answers next:

> ¹¹ He received the sign of circumcision as a seal of the righteousness that he had by faith while he was still uncircumcised. The purpose was to make him the father of all who believe without being circumcised, so that righteousness would be counted to them as well, ¹² and to make him the father of the circumcised who are not merely circumcised but who also walk in the footsteps of the faith that our father Abraham had before he was circumcised. (4:11–12)

✝ According to what Paul writes in verses 11–12, in what way was God's promise to Abraham fulfilled? Once again, here is the promise: "Look toward heaven, and number the stars, if you are able to number them. . . . So shall your offspring be" (Genesis 15:5).

4. GRACE-DEPENDENT (4:13–25)

In this next section Paul sums up all he's been saying—salvation is by faith alone for everyone, both Jew and Gentile.

> ¹³ For the promise to Abraham and his offspring that he would be heir of the world did not come through the law but through the righteousness of faith. ¹⁴ For if it is the adherents of the law who are to be the heirs, faith is null and the promise is void. ¹⁵ For the law brings wrath, but where there is no law there is no transgression. (4:14–15)

The reason God's law brings wrath is that no one is able to keep it! Facing up to the reality of our inadequacy helps us understand what Paul says next:

> ¹⁶ That is why it depends on faith, in order that the promise may rest on grace and be guaranteed to all his offspring—not only to the adherent of the law [the Jew] but also to the one [the non-Jew] who shares the faith of Abraham, who is

the father of us all, ¹⁷ as it is written, "I have made you the father of many nations"—in the presence of the God in whom he believed, who gives life to the dead and calls into existence the things that do not exist. (4:16–17)

It's all grace! That's Paul's point. The gift of salvation—of faith itself—comes to us by grace, which, we recall, is God's mercy and blessing given to those who deserve only wrath. And here we begin to get a glimpse inside the faith of Abraham himself, why he trusted God's promise of offspring even though Abraham was long past child-bearing years: God can create life where no chance of life exists.

Paul takes us deeper into Abraham's faith as he continues:

> ¹⁸ In hope he believed against hope, that he should become the father of many nations, as he had been told, "So shall your offspring be." ¹⁹ He did not weaken in faith when he considered his own body, which was as good as dead (since he was about a hundred years old), or when he considered the barrenness of Sarah's womb. ²⁰ No unbelief made him waver concerning the promise of God, but he grew strong in his faith as he gave glory to God, ²¹ fully convinced that God was able to do what he had promised. ²² That is why his faith was "counted to him as righteousness." (4:18–22)

✦ What had the potential to turn Abraham's faith toward unbelief?

✦ How did Abraham strengthen his faith as he waited (fourteen years!) for God to keep his promise?

Paul concludes this section with a beautiful summary of the gospel:

> ²³ But the words "it was counted to him" were not written for his sake alone, but for ours also. It will be counted to us who believe in him who raised from the dead Jesus our Lord, who was delivered up for our trespasses and raised for our justification. (4:23–25)

LET'S TALK

1. Why do you think that the faith of the gospel can reside only in a humble heart? Talk about why a "boasting" heart, a self-reliant one, cannot embrace the gospel.

....

....

....

....

....

....

2. Do you struggle with guilt? Sometimes it's a weight we just can't seem to shake. King David struggled with guilt, as we saw this week when Paul quotes Psalm 32. Look back at the quote in Romans 4:7–8 and discuss what you see in those verses that freed David from this burden. If you have time, you might want to take a look at Psalm 32 in its entirety and talk about how the psalm reflects your personal experience.

....

....

....

3. Abraham focused on God and his promises rather than on his circumstances—a beautiful picture of active faith. How does his example strengthen your own faith, either in a particular circumstance or in general?

WEEK 4

A BRAND-NEW REALITY

ROMANS 5:1–21

Let's face it—we all struggle with insecurity in one way or another, and that's because our lives on this earth *aren't* secure. Health and wealth come and go, relationships slip away, and no matter how hard we fight for tranquility, we just can't hold on to it. But when we're united to Christ, we can let go of our frantic attempts to make life work the way we imagine it should. He has secured for us every blessing that really matters. Beginning here in Romans 5, the apostle Paul unfolds these great blessings. In Christ we have peace, unlimited access to God, an abundance of his grace, and hope that won't let us down.

1. REASONS TO REJOICE (5:1–5)

We are justified—declared righteous in God's eyes—when, by faith, we recognize that we can do nothing to earn God's favor and gladly take hold of all Christ did for us. God placed our sin on Jesus, and placed Christ's righteousness on us. Now, clothed in the righteousness of Christ, we are accepted by God. A justified sinner can never be condemned. And being justified by God is a one-time occurrence. Once God has made that declaration over us, it's set for eternity. We never have to worry that God will change his mind, and we can joyfully embrace all the blessings that come along with it.

> ¹Therefore, since we have been justified by faith, we have peace with God through our Lord Jesus Christ. ²Through him we have also obtained access by faith into

this grace in which we stand, and we rejoice in hope of the glory of God. ³ Not only that, but we rejoice in our sufferings, knowing that suffering produces endurance, ⁴ and endurance produces character, and character produces hope, ⁵ and hope does not put us to shame, because God's love has been poured into our hearts through the Holy Spirit who has been given to us. (vv. 1–5)

✧ Note what we learn in this passage about the blessings of peace, grace, and hope:

- peace:

- grace:

- hope:

✧ How does each person of the Trinity—Father, Son, and Holy Spirit—carry out a distinctive role in conveying these blessings to us?

- God the Father:

- Christ the Son:

- The Holy Spirit:

✦ Why does Paul say that we can actually rejoice in our sufferings?

Hope factors immensely into the blessings we receive in Christ. When Paul writes of hope that won't shame us in the long run, he means that what God intends to accomplish through our suffering will surely happen. Believers can take comfort in knowing that whatever they suffer is increasing their capacity to know and enjoy God.

2. TRUE LOVE (5:6–11)

Now Paul lays out the reason we can be confident in God's love and in receiving all the blessings he's just described:

> ⁶ For while we were still weak, at the right time Christ died for the ungodly. ⁷ For one will scarcely die for a righteous person—though perhaps for a good person one would dare even to die—⁸ but God shows his love for us in that while we were still sinners, Christ died for us. ⁹ Since, therefore, we have now been justified by his blood, much more shall we be saved by him from the wrath of God. ¹⁰ For if while we were enemies we were reconciled to God by the death

of his Son, much more, now that we are reconciled, shall we be saved by his life. ¹¹More than that, we also rejoice in God through our Lord Jesus Christ, through whom we have now received reconciliation. (vv. 6–11)

✦ List all the words you see in this passage about the nature of human beings. What do these characteristics about humans reveal about God's love?

....

....

....

....

✦ We understand that Christ's death on the cross paid the debt we each owe to God for our sin, but our guilty *status* isn't the only change. What other change does Paul emphasize in this passage?

....

....

....

....

Adam and Eve had enjoyed perfect harmony with God in the garden of Eden, but when they sinned, their relationship with him was broken—not only for Adam and Eve but for every human being afterward. (You can read the tragic story in Genesis 3:1–19.) But through the cross Jesus did what no mere human could—reconcile the irreconcilable. A reconciled relationship is one that has been restored to its former harmony following a relational fracture. This is how Paul describes the Christian's relationship with God—reconciled.

Twice in this passage, in verses 9 and 10, Paul speaks of salvation in a future sort of way: "... much more *shall* we be saved." Let's be sure we understand. He's *not* saying that our justification is somehow incomplete. Rather, he has in mind the full and final result of our being justified—participating with the resurrected Lord Jesus in heavenly joys for all eternity.

✦ As we get to the end of the passage, we see where all these blessings are meant to reorient our hearts. How is that reorientation described in verse 11?

3. THE BETTER ADAM (5:12-19)

We touched on Adam and Eve when we looked at verses 6–11, how their sin in the garden of Eden broke relational harmony with God, not only for them but for every human being born after them. But that's not all sin did, as we see now, when Paul brings Adam's sin, what theologians call "the fall," front and center:

> ¹²Therefore, just as sin came into the world through one man, and death through sin, and so death spread to all men because all sinned—¹³for sin indeed was in the world before the law was given, but sin is not counted where there is no law. ¹⁴Yet death reigned from Adam to Moses, even over those whose sinning was not like the transgression of Adam, who was a type of the one who was to come. (vv. 12–14)

✦ Verse 12 is a short summary of what happened in Genesis 3:1–19. Review those verses in Genesis and jot down a sentence or two about how sin resulted in death, both spiritual and physical.

You're not alone if you find Romans 5:14 a bit confusing at first. In this verse, Paul is merely refining what he's just written about how Adam's sin impacted the entire human race. When Paul says that "death reigned from Adam to Moses," he's referring to the time that passed—the generations—from the fall to when God delivered his law to Moses. Adam, the first man, violated God's specific instruction about the fruit tree in the garden. Although the people born after him weren't guilty of that same violation, they were equally guilty of their own sin because, as his descendants, they inherited Adam's sin nature. But verse 14 isn't all doom and gloom. Adam, as the first man, was a "type," a foreshadow, of one who was to come later, the second Adam, Jesus Christ. "All people are either 'in Adam' or 'in Christ.' . . . All are in Adam by physical birth, while only those with the new birth are in Christ."[15]

This is deep theological stuff. It's challenging, but it's so worth the effort. And consider the fact that diving deeply into these things is what makes you a theologian! So be encouraged to press ahead as we watch Paul unfold more details of the gospel:

> [15] But the free gift is not like the trespass. For if many died through one man's trespass, much more have the grace of God and the free gift by the grace of that one man Jesus Christ abounded for many. [16] And the free gift is not like the result of that one man's sin. For the judgment following one trespass brought condemnation, but the free gift following many trespasses brought justification. [17] For if, because of one man's trespass, death reigned through that one man, much more will those who receive the abundance of grace and the free gift of righteousness reign in life through the one man Jesus Christ. [18] Therefore, as one trespass led to condemnation for all men, so one act of righteousness leads to justification and life for all men. [19] For as by the one man's disobedience the many were made sinners, so by the one man's obedience the many will be made righteous. (vv. 15–19)

✦ What words does Paul use repeatedly in verses 15–17 to indicate how we receive the gospel?

✦ In verses 15–19, Paul makes comparisons between what we inherit from the first Adam and what we inherit from the "second Adam," Jesus Christ. Draw out these comparisons in the "Inheritance" chart on page 41.

Inheritance

	Inheritance in Adam	Inheritance in Christ
v. 15		
v. 16		
v. 17		
v. 18		
v. 19		

4. GRACE ABOUNDING (5:20–21)

Paul makes one final contrast, this one between law and grace:

> [20] Now the law came in to increase the trespass, but where sin increased, grace abounded all the more, [21] so that, as sin reigned in death, grace also might reign through righteousness leading to eternal life through Jesus Christ our Lord. (vv. 20–21)

So why did God give the law, if it put sinners in even more danger of God's wrath? We find our answer in the gospel. God set a purposefully impossible standard so that people would realize they can't be righteous. This isn't the first time we've noted this truth in our study. The law was given to expose our total inability to obey God. No one can truly obey the law, and this means that everyone deserves the penalty for law-breakers, which is death. So what are we to do? We must turn to the righteousness of the only one who could—and did: Jesus Christ. The law was given to expose our lawlessness so that we'd turn to God for mercy.

> *"We may think at times that we have sought God. But as we grow in grace and increasingly learn the nature of our own sinful hearts, we discover that we have sought him only because he first sought us."*[16]

With that in mind, what do you think Paul means when he writes that "where sin increased, grace abounded all the more"?

LET'S TALK

1. We can rejoice even when we suffer, because through our difficulties, God is maturing our character, and as we mature, our capacity for hope is enlarged. Discuss how this has happened in your own life, even in the smallest of ways. Talk too about hope in general. What gives you a sense of hope? A way to know where your hope lies is by considering the opposite—what brings you disappointment.

2. Paul writes in verse 11 that we "rejoice in God through our Lord Jesus Christ." He doesn't command us to rejoice here; he assumes that we do because of all the blessings we have in Christ. Are you characterized by joy, and do you rejoice in the great blessings of salvation? Discuss what hinders your joy.

3. A wise pastor once said, "Grace always gives, but sin always takes away."[17] How have you experienced the truth of these words?

> "Grace says, 'What do you need? Tell me. Tell me anything at all.' And then grace provides that need in accord with God's perfect wisdom, invincible power, and unlimited supply."[18]

WEEK 5

SET FREE!

ROMANS 6:1–7:25

Our salvation is assured, not because we are sinless but because Christ was, and his righteousness covers us—even when we continue to struggle. The apostle Paul has been driving this point home as he seeks to show us our spiritual security in Christ. He has just finished explaining that grace trumps sin: "Where sin increased, grace abounded all the more," he wrote in 5:20. Hearing this, some might think that they can sin all they want since sin merely provides more opportunity for God to showcase his grace. But to live that way is an abuse of grace, which Paul clarifies for us this week. The bottom line is, if we truly grasp the grace we've been given, we'll hate sin more and more and turn away from it. Even so—even as believers who hate sin—we still fall into it. Our struggle against temptation so often seems like two steps forward and one back (sometimes two or three steps back). Slow or seemingly delayed progress in Christian growth can discourage us at times and even threaten our assurance that we've been saved. If your battles with sin are making you question your place in Christ, you'll find fresh encouragement in this portion of Romans.

1. FROM DEATH TO LIFE (6:1–11)

So, if God's grace is proportionately greater than our sin (look back at 5:20), why not sin? The question seems logical, doesn't it? Anticipating that some of his readers will ask this, Paul heads off the question with an immediate answer:

> ¹What shall we say then? Are we to continue in sin that grace may abound? ²By no means! How can we who died to sin still live in it? ³Do you not know

that all of us who have been baptized into Christ Jesus were baptized into his death? ⁴ We were buried therefore with him by baptism into death, in order that, just as Christ was raised from the dead by the glory of the Father, we too might walk in newness of life. ⁵ For if we have been united with him in a death like his, we shall certainly be united with him in a resurrection like his. (6:1–5)

✞ Once we've been united to Christ by faith, everything about us changes. From these verses (6:1–5), what has happened to us to bring about this change?

✞ What do you think it means to "walk in newness of life" (6:4)?

When Jesus died, he took us with him, spiritually speaking, and then we were raised with him too. Paul explains what this means practically, how this new life—the new us!—reshapes the way we live:

> ⁶ We know that our old self was crucified with him in order that the body of sin might be brought to nothing, so that we would no longer be enslaved to sin. ⁷ For one who has died has been set free from sin. ⁸ Now if we have died with Christ, we believe that we will also live with him. ⁹ We know that Christ, being raised from the dead, will never die again; death no longer has dominion over him. ¹⁰ For the death he died he died to sin, once for all, but the life he lives he lives to God. ¹¹ So you also must consider yourselves dead to sin and alive to God in Christ Jesus. (6:6–11)

Romans 6:1–7:25

✦ How does our relationship with sin change when we come to Christ?

✦ Paul instructs us in verse 11 to see ourselves through the lens of our new position in Christ: "Consider yourselves dead to sin and alive to God." How can such a viewpoint shape the way we live and the choices we make?

Spiritually speaking, being united to Christ makes us completely different people living in a completely different realm under a completely different rule. Formerly we were dead in sin, but now we are alive to God; formerly we were tied to this world, but now we are joined to Christ; formerly we loved to obey sin, Satan, and worldly powers, but now we long to obey God and live in his ways. The change hasn't been perfected in us yet, but if we're in Christ, we can be sure it's happening.

2. KICK IT OUT! (6:12–14)

When temptation is especially strong, it can seem like we have no choice but to sin, but Paul exposes why it doesn't have to be that way:

> ¹² Let not sin therefore reign in your mortal body, to make you obey its passions. ¹³ Do not present your members to sin as instruments for unrighteousness, but present yourselves to God as those who have been brought from death to life, and your members to God as instruments for righteousness. ¹⁴ For sin will have no dominion over you, since you are not under law but under grace. (6:12–14)

✦ Paul gives a four-part command in verses 12 and 13 to keep us from sinning. Identify each of the four parts.

1. _____

2. _____

3. _____

4. _____

✦ According to verse 12, what happens if we are careless about dealing with our sins?

_____

_____

_____

_____

✦ What promise are we given in verse 14 that obedience to God is always possible?

_____

_____

_____

_____

3. SLAVES OF RIGHTEOUSNESS (6:15–23)

For anyone still wrestling with the mistaken idea that God's grace gives license to sin, Paul strengthens his argument:

> ¹⁵ What then? Are we to sin because we are not under law but under grace? By no means! ¹⁶ Do you not know that if you present yourselves to anyone as obedient slaves, you are slaves of the one whom you obey, either of sin, which leads to death, or of obedience, which leads to righteousness? ¹⁷ But thanks be to God, that you who were once slaves of sin have become obedient from the heart to the standard of teaching to which you were committed, ¹⁸ and, having

been set free from sin, have become slaves of righteousness. ⁱ⁹ I am speaking in human terms, because of your natural limitations. For just as you once presented your members as slaves to impurity and to lawlessness leading to more lawlessness, so now present your members as slaves to righteousness leading to sanctification. (6:15–19)

✢ How, according to Paul, does someone become enslaved, whether to sin or to righteousness?

✢ Slavery is defined as "submission to a dominating influence."¹⁹ What does this slave imagery teach us about the way sin affects the choices we make?

✢ Paul reminds believers that they were "once slaves of sin" but have "become obedient from the heart" and "slaves of righteousness" (6:17–18). As you think back on all Paul has written so far in the letter, note again here what produces this change.

To encourage us in our fight against sin, Paul wants us to reflect on life before we were saved in Christ:

> ²⁰ For when you were slaves of sin, you were free in regard to righteousness. ²¹ But what fruit were you getting at that time from the things of which you are now ashamed? For the end of those things is death. ²² But now that you have been set free from sin and have become slaves of God, the fruit you get leads to sanctification and its end, eternal life. ²³ For the wages of sin is death, but the free gift of God is eternal life in Christ Jesus our Lord. (6:20–23)

✠ Notice the words Paul uses for what sin is and does and how he contrasts sin with Christ's righteousness. Note the distinctions in the "Fruit of Sin, Fruit of Salvation" chart.

	Fruit of Sin	Fruit of Salvation
6:20		
6:21		
6:22		
6:23		

✠ Now summarize this passage by completing these sentences:

Slavery to sin leads to _____

Slavery to God leads to _____

4. RELEASED (7:1-6)

As we grow in our Christian faith, where does Old Testament law—summarized in the Ten Commandments—fit into our lives? If you aren't sure, you're not alone. We know that Christ paid our penalty for sin when he died on the cross. All the sins we had ever committed were paid for there. But what about now? The reality is, we still sin. And God's law—obeying in thought, word, and deed—is still the law. So what does this mean for us now? That's what Paul deals with here, and he sets up his answer with an illustration from marriage:

> ¹Or do you not know, brothers—for I am speaking to those who know the law—that the law is binding on a person only as long as he lives? ² For a married woman is bound by law to her husband while he lives, but if her husband dies she is released from the law of marriage. ³ Accordingly, she will be called an adulteress if she lives with another man while her husband is alive. But if her husband dies, she is free from that law, and if she marries another man she is not an adulteress.
> ⁴ Likewise, my brothers, you also have died to the law through the body of Christ, so that you may belong to another, to him who has been raised from the dead, in order that we may bear fruit for God. (7:1–4)

✢ The demands of the law itself haven't changed—God requires the death penalty for those who fail to obey it perfectly. But Christians are no longer under this penalty. Why is the penalty for lawbreakers no longer "binding" for Christians?

✢ What does Paul's illustration reveal about the nature of a believer's relationship with Christ?

Apart from Christ, human beings can't manage God's law. No one can keep it, and, in fact, it actually provokes people to sin even more.

> [5] For while we were living in the flesh, our sinful passions, aroused by the law, were at work in our members to bear fruit for death. [6] But now we are released from the law, having died to that which held us captive, so that we serve in the new way of the Spirit and not in the old way of the written code. (7:5–6)

✢ Freedom from the law doesn't mean freedom from serving. How does Paul make this distinction in verse 6?

5. THE CRUX OF THE PROBLEM (7:7–13)

Paul continues teaching about Christians' relationship to the law, illustrating this time from his personal story:

> [7] What then shall we say? That the law is sin? By no means! Yet if it had not been for the law, I would not have known sin. For I would not have known what it is to covet if the law had not said, "You shall not covet." [8] But sin, seizing an opportunity through the commandment, produced in me all kinds of covetousness. For apart from the law, sin lies dead. [9] I was once alive apart from the law, but when the commandment came, sin came alive and I died. [10] The very commandment that promised life proved to be death to me. [11] For sin, seizing an opportunity through the commandment, deceived me and through it killed me. [12] So the law is holy, and the commandment is holy and righteous and good. [13] Did that which is good, then, bring death to me? By no means! It was sin, producing death in me through what is good, in order that sin might be shown to be sin, and through the commandment might become sinful beyond measure. (7:7–13)

The law itself isn't bad—in fact, it is "holy and righteous and good." God's law is an instrument, a searchlight of sorts that exposes what's in someone's heart. That's what Paul means when he says that "apart from the law, sin lies dead."

✦ Before his conversion to Christ, Paul had been a well-regarded Pharisee. Pharisees were devout Jews who prided themselves on knowing and keeping God's law. They trusted in their personal righteousness for salvation, and they looked down on those who didn't. This is what Paul is remembering when he writes, "I was once alive apart from the law." But the Spirit used the law to penetrate Paul's heart. How did this happen for Paul?

Coveting is forbidden in the tenth commandment: "You shall not covet your neighbor's house; you shall not covet your neighbor's wife, or his male servant, or his female servant, or his ox, or his donkey, or anything that is your neighbor's" (Exodus 20:17). We covet whenever we want what others have badly enough to take it away from them. Compared to sins like murder and adultery (also forbidden in the Ten Commandments), coveting doesn't seem so bad. After all, if we don't act on it, who does it harm? But Paul's words here indicate that it is a really big deal because it violates God's law from the heart.

6. DOING WHAT WE HATE (7:14–25)

So the law was instrumental in bringing Paul to see his hopeless condition and his need for the salvation that comes only through Christ by faith. The law convicted him of sin, but it didn't condemn him because Christ paid his penalty on the cross. That's true of all Christians. We are justified—declared not guilty—forever. But though the penalty of sin has been permanently removed, its presence lingers:

> ¹⁴ For we know that the law is spiritual, but I am of the flesh, sold under sin. ¹⁵ For I do not understand my own actions. For I do not do what I want, but I do the very thing I hate. ¹⁶ Now if I do what I do not want, I agree with the law, that it is good. ¹⁷ So now it is no longer I who do it, but sin that dwells within me. ¹⁸ For I know that nothing good dwells in me, that is, in my flesh. For I have the desire to do what is right, but not the ability to carry it out. ¹⁹ For I do not do the good I want, but the evil I do not want is what I keep on

> doing. ²⁰ Now if I do what I do not want, it is no longer I who do it, but sin that dwells within me. ²¹ So I find it to be a law that when I want to do right, evil lies close at hand. (7:14–21)

Once we have been united to Christ, never again will God hold our sin against us. And the fact is, we still sin as we live out our faith in day-to-day life. Throughout this time, from our conversion until we are taken home to heaven, God sanctifies us. The word *sanctify* means "set apart," and it's used by theologians to refer to the Lord's transforming work in our lives. Unlike our once-for-all-time justification, sanctification is a lifelong process. As we live out our faith in everyday life, God is slowly but surely changing us to resemble and reflect our Lord Jesus.

✢ What picture does 7:14–21 paint of the normal Christian life?

✢ According to verse 17, what is the reason for the conflict we face as we grow up in our faith?

Now Paul summarizes his experience—and our experience too—of the Christian life:

> ²² For I delight in the law of God, in my inner being, ²³ but I see in my members another law waging war against the law of my mind and making me captive to the law of sin that dwells in my members. ²⁴ Wretched man that I am! Who will deliver me from this body of death? ²⁵ Thanks be to God through Jesus Christ our Lord! So then, I myself serve the law of God with my mind, but with my flesh I serve the law of sin. (7:22–25)

✦ Before we are saved, we don't care about pleasing God. What in us changes when we are united to Christ?

✦ When our struggle with sin feels especially difficult, why can we be confident that sin won't have the last word?

LET'S TALK

1. You are promised that "sin will have no dominion over you, since you are not under law but under grace" (6:14). How does having this promise empower you in your fight against sin?

2. We are all tempted to sin, but we're not all tempted by the same sins. What's easy for one to avoid might be very difficult for another. All the same, we likely do share in common a struggle to overcome a particular sin or sins, sometimes called "besetting" sins. Rather than a once-for-all rejection of the sin, we find ourselves taking two steps forward and one back—a frustrating experience! Paul shares his own struggle: "I do not do the good I want, but the evil I do not want is what I keep on doing" (7:19). From him we learn that this is a normal aspect of the Christian life. How does knowing of Paul's struggle encourage you in your battle?

3. This section of the epistle is a "blueprint" for how we are gradually transformed to reflect our Savior's holiness, the process theologians call "sanctification." How has your understanding of sanctification changed as you've studied this lesson?

WEEK 6

YOUR BEST LIFE NOW— AND ALWAYS

ROMANS 8:1-39

No condemnation! That's the reality for everyone who's united to Christ by faith. Nothing we've done or will do will ever again change God's determination to bless us and bring us safely home to heaven. This eighth chapter of the epistle not only assures us that we'll reach our eternal destiny but also empowers us to live confidently until we get there. This week we see how God uses even our griefs and trials to bless us and how he turns every bad thing into something good for his people. We also get vital insights about running hard after holiness, and we find a lot of encouragement for our prayer life. Here, more than anywhere else in the letter, we see how the Holy Spirit works in us and for us. All these things—every blessing held out to us in this chapter—are rooted in God's unshakable love for us in Christ Jesus.

1. LIFE IN THE SPIRIT (8:1-11)

Christians still struggle with sin, but it no longer defines them:

> ¹There is therefore now no condemnation for those who are in Christ Jesus. ²For the law of the Spirit of life has set you free in Christ Jesus from the law of sin and death. ³For God has done what the law, weakened by the flesh, could not do. By sending his own Son in the likeness of sinful flesh and for sin, he condemned sin in the flesh, ⁴in order that the righteous requirement of the law might be fulfilled in us, who walk not according to the flesh but according to the Spirit. (vv. 1–4)

Christ paid the penalty for our sin on the cross—he took on himself the condemnation that belonged to us, justifying us before God. Now that we are "in Christ Jesus," the threat of the law has no power over us, and we've been set free to live in a radically new way. Look how Paul illuminates the difference between Christians and unbelievers:

> ⁵ For those who live according to the flesh set their minds on the things of the flesh, but those who live according to the Spirit set their minds on the things of the Spirit. For to set the mind on the flesh is death, but to set the mind on the Spirit is life and peace. For the mind that is set on the flesh is hostile to God, for it does not submit to God's law; indeed, it cannot. Those who are in the flesh cannot please God. (vv. 5–8)

✤ What does this passage tell us about unbelievers?

The work of the Holy Spirit comes front and center in chapter 8. Through our union with Christ, the Spirit takes up residence within us and works to make us increasingly holy. This is what sanctification is all about.

✤ We play no part in our justification, but our participation is vital in sanctification. The Spirit works, and we cooperate with what he's doing. How is that shown in verses 5–8?

Observing the text is an important part of studying the Bible. As we observe verses 9–11, we can't help but notice the repeated use of the word *dwells*. When a word is repeated, it means we should give it special attention:

> ⁹ You, however, are not in the flesh but in the Spirit, if in fact the Spirit of God *dwells* in you. Anyone who does not have the Spirit of Christ does not belong

Romans 8:1–39

to him. ¹⁰ But if Christ is in you, although the body is dead because of sin, the Spirit is life because of righteousness. ¹¹ If the Spirit of him who raised Jesus from the dead *dwells* in you, he who raised Christ Jesus from the dead will also give life to your mortal bodies through his Spirit who *dwells* in you. (vv. 9–11)

✛ No matter how much we grow spiritually in this life, our bodies will one day die unless Christ returns before then to take us home to heaven (v. 10). Despite this inevitable end, why is there reason for hope rather than despair?

✛ It's so clear here in these verses that all three persons of the Trinity—Father, Son, and Holy Spirit—are involved in our salvation and ongoing transformation. Note what is said about each person:

- Father:

- Son:

- Holy Spirit:

Here's a helpful way to apply these deep spiritual truths practically: *"Through the process of sanctification, we are to live cognizant of the fact that God dwells personally and permanently within us. Because this is so, living in a way that is contrary to Him will be a most miserable condition for us. It will be to live in opposition to the God who inhabits His people, which will rob us of our joy, comfort, and communion with Him."*[20]

> *"Along with Christ, and the Holy Spirit, God the Father dwells in us, for where the One is, the others are always present."*[21]

2. HEIRS OF LIFE (8:12–17)

All the spiritual truths Paul has been showing us are meant to shape the way we live. That's what we come to now:

> [12] So then, brothers, we are debtors, not to the flesh, to live according to the flesh. [13] For if you live according to the flesh you will die, but if by the Spirit you put to death the deeds of the body, you will live. [14] For all who are led by the Spirit of God are sons of God. [15] For you did not receive the spirit of slavery to fall back into fear, but you have received the Spirit of adoption as sons, by whom we cry, "Abba! Father!" [16] The Spirit himself bears witness with our spirit that we are children of God, [17] and if children, then heirs—heirs of God and fellow heirs with Christ, provided we suffer with him in order that we may also be glorified with him. (vv. 12–17)

✦ Once again, the Spirit is front and center in the work of sanctification. What do you learn about the Spirit's sanctifying work in each of the following verses?

- v. 13

- v. 14

- v. 15

- v. 16

✦ What do you think it means practically to live according to the Spirit rather than the flesh? (You might want to take a look at Galatians 5:16–26.)

✦ As God's children, we inherit all the promises that God's firstborn Son, our Lord Jesus, has inherited. What does verse 17 mark out as an indicator of our right to inherit?

3. THE BEST IS YET TO COME (8:18–25)

From the moment we're saved, we begin to enjoy all the blessings of our union with Christ, but we continue to experience the suffering that accompanies life in a fallen world:

> ¹⁸ For I consider that the sufferings of this present time are not worth comparing with the glory that is to be revealed to us. ¹⁹ For the creation waits with eager longing for the revealing of the sons of God. ²⁰ For the creation was subjected to futility, not willingly, but because of him who subjected it, in hope ²¹ that the creation itself will be set free from its bondage to corruption and obtain the freedom of the glory of the children of God. ²² For we know that the whole creation has been groaning together in the pains of childbirth until now. ²³ And not only the creation, but we ourselves, who have the firstfruits of the Spirit, groan inwardly as we wait eagerly for adoption as sons, the redemption of our bodies. ²⁴ For in this hope we were saved. Now hope that is seen is not hope. For who hopes for what he sees? ²⁵ But if we hope for what we do not see, we wait for it with patience. (vv. 18–25)

✦ How can Paul's mindset in verse 18 shape our view of suffering and encourage perseverance?

✦ Before Adam and Eve sinned, life in the garden of Eden was perfect. Everything God made flourished in harmony. When sin entered, all that changed. Plants and animals and all creation were negatively affected by human sin. God told Adam, "Cursed is the ground because of you; in pain you shall eat of it all the days of your life; thorns and thistles it shall bring forth for you" (Genesis 3:17–18). Paul reflects on sin's marring of creation here in Romans 8. How do the following passages help us understand the hope Paul anticipates?

- Isaiah 11:6–9

- 1 Corinthians 15:19–26, 42–49, 51–58

The Golden Chain of Romans 8		
	Meaning	Timing
Foreknew (v. 29)	God's choice of specific individuals	Eternal
Predestined (v. 29)	God's determination to save his chosen ones	Eternal
Called (v. 30)	God's irresistible drawing of hearts by the Spirit to Christ	In time
Justified (v. 30)	God's declaring individuals "not guilty" and at the same time applying to them the perfect righteousness of Christ	In time
Glorified (v. 30)	God's perfecting of those he has called, both spiritually and physically	Already assured but fully realized when Christ returns

- Revelation 22:1–5

Paul is honest about our "inward groaning" as we wait for future glory, our "adoption as sons, the redemption of our bodies" (Romans 8:22–23). In Christ we have already been adopted—permanently—into God's family. He is speaking here about the time when everything that accompanies our adoption is completed in heaven.

4. ALL FOR GOOD (8:26-30)

We see still more of the Spirit's work on behalf of believers and what his work is accomplishing in us:

> ²⁶ Likewise the Spirit helps us in our weakness. For we do not know what to pray for as we ought, but the Spirit himself intercedes for us with groanings too deep for words. ²⁷ And he who searches hearts knows what is the mind of the Spirit, because the Spirit intercedes for the saints according to the will of God. ²⁸ And we know that for those who love God all things work together for good, for those who are called according to his purpose. ²⁹ For those whom he foreknew he also predestined to be conformed to the image of his Son, in order that he might be the firstborn among many brothers. ³⁰ And those whom he predestined he also called, and those whom he called he also justified, and those whom he justified he also glorified. (vv. 26–30)

✣ The Spirit is intimately involved in our prayers. How can verses 26–27 shape or reshape the way we pray?

Romans 8:1–39

✦ In verse 28 Paul assures believers that all things work together for their good. According to verses 29–30, how are we meant to understand this wonderful promise?

....

....

....

....

....

....

✦ The blessings of salvation named in verses 29–30 are sometimes called "the golden chain" of salvation. (If you aren't sure of the meaning of the terms used here, see "The Golden Chain" chart on p. 63.) The order in which these blessings appear isn't random—it's very purposeful. List these blessings in the order they appear:

1. ....
2. ....
3. ....
4. ....
5. ....

> ### Finding God's Will
>
> "We do not need to be under pressure to 'discover' it, fearing that if we miss it, somehow we will be doomed to a life outside the center of God's will or to his 'second best.' We are free to make decisions with what light and wisdom we possess. Nevertheless, we can know that God does have a perfect will for us, that the Holy Spirit is praying for us in accordance with that will, and that this will of God for us will be done."[22]

✤ What do you learn from this "golden chain" about your own salvation?

✤ According to verse 29, what is God's overarching purpose for bringing us to himself?

Sanctification isn't explicitly stated in the golden chain, but it is certainly woven in here. It's the unwritten blessing that begins the moment we are justified until we are glorified. So although our spiritual progress seems slow, we can be sure it's happening!

5. GOD'S OVER-THE-TOP LOVE (8:31–39)

There are times we echo Paul's frustrated cry, "Wretched man that I am!" (7:24). We know what it's like to carry out with our flesh what we hate in our spirit, and we long for the battle to cease. Although the conflict won't end until heaven, we can be sure of final victory:

> ³¹ What then shall we say to these things? If God is for us, who can be against us? ³² He who did not spare his own Son but gave him up for us all, how will he not also with him graciously give us all things? ³³ Who shall bring any charge against God's elect? It is God who justifies. ³⁴ Who is to condemn? Christ Jesus is the one who died—more than that, who was raised—who is at the right hand of God, who indeed is interceding for us. ³⁵ Who shall separate us from the love of Christ? Shall tribulation, or distress, or persecution, or famine, or nakedness, or danger, or sword? ³⁶ As it is written,
>
> > "For your sake we are being killed all the day long;
> > we are regarded as sheep to be slaughtered."

Romans 8:1–39

> ³⁷ No, in all these things we are more than conquerors through him who loved us. ³⁸ For I am sure that neither death nor life, nor angels nor rulers, nor things present nor things to come, nor powers, ³⁹ nor height nor depth, nor anything else in all creation, will be able to separate us from the love of God in Christ Jesus our Lord. (vv. 31–39)

In addition to battling sin, we face all the varied sufferings of life in a fallen world, which Paul indicates in verse 39 when he quotes from Psalm 44. Although the outcome is sure, we need help for the battlefield.

✣ After meditating on verses 31–39, write down in your own words the answers to the questions Paul asks:

- Who can be against us? (v. 31)

  ....
  ....
  ....

- What can we count on God to give us? (v. 32)

  ....
  ....
  ....

- Who can condemn us for sin? (vv. 33–34)

  ....
  ....
  ....

- What can negatively affect Christ's love for us? (vv. 35–39)

  ....
  ....
  ....

✦ What is the ultimate guarantee that we will make it home to heaven?

LET'S TALK

1. Romans 8:13 tells us that by the Spirit we must "put to death the deeds of the body." Unlike our justification, which we play no part in, we play an active role in our sanctification, our progressive transformation into holy women. Talk about this cooperative work, what the Spirit does and what we are to do. How do we "put to death" our sinful cravings and desires? You might find Philippians 2:12–13 helpful here.

2. The apostle says bluntly that we don't know the right way to pray, and then he explains why our weakness with prayer doesn't hinder God from answering us (Romans 8:26–27). Name an area of your life for which you find this understanding of prayer especially encouraging.

3. God's will for our lives is revealed in verses 28–30. Talk about how this changes your view of a troublesome circumstance you're currently dealing with.

WEEK 7

ALL HEARTS IN GOD'S HANDS

ROMANS 9:1-33

We come now to what is for some the most difficult portion of Romans. Here in chapter 9 Paul goes back to where he began—reaching out to his fellow Jews. Gentiles have come flooding into the church. At the same time, a large number of Jews, God's people Israel, have rejected Jesus. Because of this rejection, Paul says, these Jews are now the outsiders, and therefore, to their way of thinking, God has failed to keep his covenant promise. But the truth is, they have misunderstood that promise, and that's what Paul explains here in Romans 9. Chapters 9–11 are actually a single section of the letter, one unit, but because some aspects of chapter 9 are especially challenging to understand, we're going to devote this entire week to just this portion. Let me urge you before we begin not to be put off by Paul's focus on the Jews, as if everyone else was excluded from what he's teaching here. The truth is, what's here is for all God's people, including us. In this section we get to see how God works through centuries and people and even emotions to bring about his purposes. We get to see that his promises never fail. And we get to see that God determines the destiny of every human being. So, as you can see, all this matters a great deal for each one of us.

1. DOES GOD KEEP HIS PROMISES? (9:1-13)

If you have loved ones who aren't saved, you'll understand the anguish Paul expresses here about his fellow Jews:

> ¹I am speaking the truth in Christ—I am not lying; my conscience bears me witness in the Holy Spirit—²that I have great sorrow and unceasing anguish in my heart. ³For I could wish that I myself were accursed and cut off from Christ for the sake of my brothers, my kinsmen according to the flesh. ⁴They are Israelites, and to them belong the adoption, the glory, the covenants, the giving of the law, the worship, and the promises. ⁵To them belong the patriarchs, and from their race, according to the flesh, is the Christ, who is God over all, blessed forever. Amen. (vv. 1–5)

✝ The majority of Jews in Paul's day rejected Christ as the long-promised Messiah. Based on Paul's words, what makes this rejection particularly tragic?

The Jews being cut off by their unbelief raises a perplexing question for those who know Bible history: Hadn't God called set-apart Israel, the Jewish people, to be his special people from the time of Abraham? Hadn't God brought them out of Egypt and established them in the promised land of Canaan? Hadn't he given them King David and the promise of David's descendants to keep them forever secure? So, if the Jews have now been cut off by not believing in Jesus, doesn't that mean God's promises to Israel have failed? Here's how Paul answers:

> ⁶But it is not as though the word of God has failed. For not all who are descended from Israel belong to Israel, ⁷and not all are children of Abraham because they are his offspring, but "Through Isaac shall your offspring be named." ⁸This means that it is not the children of the flesh who are the children of God, but the children of the promise are counted as offspring. ⁹For this is what the promise said: "About this time next year I will return, and Sarah shall have a son." ¹⁰And not only so, but also when Rebekah had conceived children by one man, our forefather Isaac, ¹¹though they were not yet born and had done nothing either good or bad—in order that God's purpose of election might continue, not because of works but because of him who calls—¹²she was told, "The older will serve the younger." ¹³As it is written, "Jacob I loved, but Esau I hated." (vv. 6–13)

Back in Genesis, God promised the patriarch Abraham and his wife Sarah a son of their very own, but they got tired of waiting for God to fulfill this promise, so they obtained a son, Ishmael, by means of a surrogate. But a son born to Abraham's true wife Sarah, a boy named Isaac, was the promised son (you'll find God's promise of this son in Genesis 18:10–15). So here Paul reminds his readers of this history. Then, to reinforce the point he's making, he includes Isaac's own sons, Esau and Jacob. According to custom, Esau as firstborn was entitled to special rights and privileges, but the younger son, Jacob, was given those blessings instead.

✜ What truth about God is Paul emphasizing through this look back at Israel's history?

2. IS GOD UNFAIR? (9:14-18)

God's choosing Jacob the younger over Esau the firstborn wasn't breaking a promise—it was fulfilling a promise in his own way. So the problem isn't that God doesn't keep his promises—it's that his people have their own expectations of how those promises should play out. But this now raises another question:

> ¹⁴ What shall we say then? Is there injustice on God's part? By no means! ¹⁵ For he says to Moses, "I will have mercy on whom I have mercy, and I will have compassion on whom I have compassion." ¹⁶ So then it depends not on human will or exertion, but on God, who has mercy. ¹⁷ For the Scripture says to Pharaoh, "For this very purpose I have raised you up, that I might show my power in you, and that my name might be proclaimed in all the earth." ¹⁸ So then he has mercy on whomever he wills, and he hardens whomever he wills. (vv. 14–18)

The question has to do with God's justice, or fairness. Paul answers by drawing from yet more of Israel's history. He first reminds his readers of how God revealed himself to Moses on Mount Sinai: "I will have mercy on whom I have mercy, and I will have compassion on whom I have compassion." (You can read the fuller story in Exodus 33.)

✦ How is the justice question answered through God's words to Moses that Paul quotes here?

Continuing to address the question about God's justice, Paul brings in Pharaoh, the Egyptian ruler who enslaved and bullied God's people in Egypt and refused to let them leave. (The full story, which is well worth the time to read, is found in Exodus 7–14.) Let's draw out just a few key things from that story that relate specifically to Paul's point here in Romans.

✦ First, what two reasons are given in Romans 9:17 for why Pharaoh came to rule?

1.
2.

Paul has used the Lord's own words to make his case for God's justice, and he summarizes his case in verse 18: "So then he has mercy on whomever he wills, and he hardens whomever he wills."

✦ Pharaoh played a huge part in Israel's history, so it makes sense that Paul illustrates his teaching with what happened to Pharaoh during the ten plagues God sent on Egypt. Study the "Pharaoh's Heart" chart on pages 75–76 and then summarize *how* Pharaoh's heart was hardened.

Romans 9:1–33

Pharaoh's Heart

The LORD said to Moses, . . . "You shall speak all that I command you, and your brother Aaron shall tell Pharaoh to let the people of Israel go out of his land. But I will harden Pharaoh's heart, and though I multiply my signs and wonders in the land of Egypt, Pharaoh will not listen to you." (Exodus 7:1-4)

	The Lord	Pharaoh
1st Plague: Water to Blood Moses and Aaron did as the LORD commanded. In the sight of Pharaoh and in the sight of his servants he lifted up the staff and struck the water in the Nile, and all the water in the Nile turned into blood. (7:20)	But the magicians of Egypt did the same by their secret arts. So *Pharaoh's heart remained hardened*, and he would not listen to them, as the LORD had said. (7:22-23)	
2nd Plague: Frogs Aaron stretched out his hand over the waters of Egypt, and the frogs came up and covered the land of Egypt. (8:6)		When Pharaoh saw that there was a respite, *he hardened his heart* and would not listen to them, as the LORD had said. (8:15)
3rd Plague: Gnats Aaron stretched out his hand with his staff and struck the dust of the earth, and there were gnats on man and beast. (8:17)	*Pharaoh's heart was hardened*, and he would not listen to them, as the LORD had said. (8:19)	
4th Plague: Flies There came great swarms of flies into the house of Pharaoh and into his servants' houses. (8:24)		And the LORD . . . removed the swarms of flies from Pharaoh, from his servants, and from his people; not one remained. But *Pharaoh hardened his heart* this time also, and did not let the people go. (8:31-32)
5th Plague: Livestock Die All the livestock of the Egyptians died, but not one of the livestock of the people of Israel died. (9:6)	But *the heart of Pharaoh was hardened*, and he did not let the people go. (9:7)	

Pharaoh's Heart

	The Lord	Pharaoh
6th Plague: Boils They took soot from the kiln and stood before Pharaoh. And Moses threw it in the air, and it became boils breaking out in sores on man and beast. (9:10)	But *the L*ORD *hardened the heart of Pharaoh*, and he did not listen to them, as the Lord had spoken to Moses. (9:12)	
7th Plague: Hail Then Moses stretched out his staff toward heaven, and the LORD sent thunder and hail, and fire ran down to the earth. And the LORD rained hail upon the land of Egypt. (9:23)		But when Pharaoh saw that the rain and the hail and the thunder had ceased, he sinned yet again and *hardened his heart*, he and his servants. (9:34)
8th Plague: Locusts The locusts came up over all the land of Egypt and settled on the whole country of Egypt, such a dense swarm of locusts as had never been before, nor ever will be again. (10:14)	But *the L*ORD *hardened Pharaoh's heart*, and he did not let the people of Israel go. (10:20)	
9th Plague: Darkness So Moses stretched out his hand toward heaven, and there was pitch darkness in all the land of Egypt three days. (10:22)	But *the L*ORD *hardened Pharaoh's heart*, and he would not let them go. (10:27)	
10th Plague: Death of Firstborn The LORD struck down all the firstborn in the land of Egypt. (12:29)	*The L*ORD *hardened the heart of Pharaoh* king of Egypt, and he pursued the people of Israel while the people of Israel were going out. (14:8)	

3. WHO'S AT FAULT? (9:19–29)

Paul anticipates that his teaching about God's justice is likely to raise objections about human responsibility. He makes his case, drawing once again from the Old Testament:

> ¹⁹ You will say to me then, "Why does he still find fault? For who can resist his will?" ²⁰ But who are you, O man, to answer back to God? Will what is molded say to its molder, "Why have you made me like this?" ²¹ Has the potter no right over the clay, to make out of the same lump one vessel for honorable use and another for dishonorable use? (vv. 19–21)

✢ In Paul's argument, the "honorable" are those God has redeemed, and the "dishonorable" are those being hardened. What is Paul teaching about God in this illustration?

_____

_____

_____

_____

Paul builds on what he's saying with words from Hosea the prophet:

> ²² What if God, desiring to show his wrath and to make known his power, has endured with much patience vessels of wrath prepared for destruction, ²³ in order to make known the riches of his glory for vessels of mercy, which he has prepared beforehand for glory—²⁴ even us whom he has called, not from the Jews only but also from the Gentiles? ²⁵ As indeed he says in Hosea,
>
> > "Those who were not my people I will call 'my people,'
> >   and her who was not beloved I will call 'beloved.'"
> > ²⁶ "And in the very place where it was said to them, 'You are not my people,'
> >   there they will be called 'sons of the living God.'" (vv. 22–26)

Hosea was married to an adulterous woman named Gomer. She abandoned her husband Hosea to live with other lovers, and the children from this broken home were given names to reflect its brokenness: "No Mercy" and "Not My People" (Hosea 1:6–9). Hosea's broken marriage pointed to the broken relationship between God and his people. Israel was cheating on him with other gods. But in the midst of all the brokenness, the Lord gave a promise: "Yet the number of the children of Israel shall be like the sand of the sea, which cannot be measured or numbered. And in the place where it was said to them, 'You are not my people,' it shall be said to them, 'Children of the living God'" (Hosea 1:10). God also said, "I will have mercy on No Mercy, and I will say to Not My People, 'You are my people'; and he shall say, 'You are my God'" (Hosea 2:23). Paul draws from Hosea to demonstrate God's mercy on Israel and on the Gentiles to be drawn in from every nation.

Potter and Clay Illustration

God is the potter, and we are the clay:

- Isaiah 29:16; 45:9; 64:8
- Jeremiah 18:1–6

Circling back to the question about whether God has kept his promise to save Israel, Paul now quotes Isaiah the prophet:

> ²⁷ And Isaiah cries out concerning Israel: "Though the number of the sons of Israel be as the sand of the sea, only a remnant of them will be saved, ²⁸ for the Lord will carry out his sentence upon the earth fully and without delay." ²⁹ And as Isaiah predicted,
>
> "If the Lord of hosts had not left us offspring,
> we would have been like Sodom
> and become like Gomorrah." (vv. 19–29)

✢ What do these words from Isaiah clarify about God's promise to save the Jewish people, Israel?

_____

_____

_____

_____

4. GOD'S WAY, OR NO WAY AT ALL (9:30–33)

So Paul has shown that God does keep his promises, but he fulfills them in his own way in his own time. And his promises are for both Israel and Gentiles:

> ³⁰ What shall we say, then? That Gentiles who did not pursue righteousness have attained it, that is, a righteousness that is by faith; ³¹ but that Israel who

pursued a law that would lead to righteousness did not succeed in reaching that law. ³²Why? Because they did not pursue it by faith, but as if it were based on works. They have stumbled over the stumbling stone, ³³as it is written,

> "Behold, I am laying in Zion a stone of stumbling, and a rock of offense;
> and whoever believes in him will not be put to shame." (vv. 30–33)

✦ What is God's way of keeping his promise to save?

✦ For whom is Jesus Christ "a stone of stumbling, and a rock of offense"?

LET'S TALK

1. God's promises never fail. That's our overarching takeaway this week. Sometimes, though, what happens in the world and in our very own lives causes us to doubt. Discuss what you learned this week about trusting God when circumstances seem to contradict his promises.

2. Discuss the doctrine of election, which Paul set out this week. How does God's hardening of a heart work in tandem with a person's hardening of her own heart? How does this doctrine reflect both God's mercy and his justice? Share any questions or difficulties this teaching might stir up in you and pray as a group for the Spirit to give you understanding.

3. How does the doctrine of election actually encourage us to share the gospel with the lost rather than make it unnecessary?

WEEK 8

MYSTERY MADE KNOWN

ROMANS 10:1–11:36

Why would anyone prefer to pay for something rather than accept it as a gift? It just makes no sense, yet it's what so many seem to prefer when it come to God's gift of salvation. They want to be able to say, "I'm going to heaven someday because I'm a good person." Being "good" is a kind of payment, a way of earning eternal life. The apostle continues to appeal to people who think that way, particularly his Jewish kinsmen who were rejecting the gospel. They wanted their own righteousness to count rather than the righteousness of someone else, Jesus Christ. They lacked the faith that gives spiritual sight. But even faith is God's gift, and Paul shows here that it's received in the heart as God's word is proclaimed. This is why evangelism matters. It's why biblical preaching matters. These are the means, the instruments, the Holy Spirit uses to tenderize hard hearts. Although the majority of the Jews refused to hear, we're reminded this week of God's promise that a remnant of these hard-hearted Jews would come to embrace the Savior. Paul speaks directly to the Gentiles this week as well. It seems they needed a humbling reminder that their inclusion in God's family is all by grace. Most of all, on display this week are the mind-boggling power and wisdom of God that work to fulfill every detail of his plans and purposes.

1. BEING "RELIGIOUS" DOESN'T COUNT (10:1-4)

Paul expresses his strong desire that Israel, his Jewish kinsmen, would embrace the Savior:

> ¹Brothers, my heart's desire and prayer to God for them is that they may be saved. For I bear them witness that they have a zeal for God, but not according to knowledge. For, being ignorant of the righteousness of God, and seeking to establish their own, they did not submit to God's righteousness. For Christ is the end of the law for righteousness to everyone who believes. (10:1–4)

✧ Why does Paul say that the Jews are shut out from salvation?

2. LOOKING FOR LOOPHOLES (10:5–21)

For the Jews seeking an excuse, they certainly cannot claim that they haven't heard the gospel:

> ⁵For Moses writes about the righteousness that is based on the law, that the person who does the commandments shall live by them. ⁶But the righteousness based on faith says, "Do not say in your heart, 'Who will ascend into heaven?'" (that is, to bring Christ down) ⁷or 'Who will descend into the abyss?'" (that is, to bring Christ up from the dead). ⁸But what does it say? "The word is near you, in your mouth and in your heart" (that is, the word of faith that we proclaim); ⁹because, if you confess with your mouth that Jesus is Lord and believe in your heart that God raised him from the dead, you will be saved. ¹⁰For with the heart one believes and is justified, and with the mouth one confesses and is saved. ¹¹For the Scripture says, "Everyone who believes in him will not be put to shame." ¹²For there is no distinction between Jew and Greek; for the same Lord is Lord of all, bestowing his riches on all who call on him. ¹³For "everyone who calls on the name of the Lord will be saved." (10:5–13)

Paul draws from something Moses said about God's word—"The word is very near you. It is in your mouth and in your heart, so that you can do it" (Deuteronomy 30:11–14)—and he applies those words to Christ here in 10:6–8.

Romans 10:1–11:36

✦ According to verses 9–10, how is saving faith evidenced?

✦ How should Paul's words here help unify the Jewish and Gentile Christians in the Roman church?

We learn a lot in the next verses about how God changes hearts:

> ¹⁴ How then will they call on him in whom they have not believed? And how are they to believe in him of whom they have never heard? And how are they to hear without someone preaching? ¹⁵ And how are they to preach unless they are sent? As it is written, "How beautiful are the feet of those who preach the good news!" ¹⁶ But they have not all obeyed the gospel. For Isaiah says, "Lord, who has believed what he has heard from us?" ¹⁷ So faith comes from hearing, and hearing through the word of Christ. ¹⁸ But I ask, have they not heard? Indeed they have, for
>
> > "Their voice has gone out to all the earth,
> >   and their words to the ends of the world." (10:14–18)

✦ Look at the questions Paul poses in verses 14–15 and answer the following questions.

- What enables someone to *call on* God?

- What enables someone to *believe* the gospel?

- What enables someone to *hear* the gospel?

- What enables someone to *preach* the gospel?

✦ What does verse 17 teach us about our efforts to share the gospel with the lost?

For centuries, Israel had been given every opportunity to hear, yet they didn't believe the word they heard. Paul quotes Isaiah 53:1 and Psalm 19:4 to make this tragic point. Israel can't excuse their unbelief by claiming they hadn't heard God's promise. So maybe a failure to understand can be blamed? Let's see:

> [19] But I ask, did Israel not understand? First Moses says,
>
>> "I will make you jealous of those who are not a nation;
>> with a foolish nation I will make you angry."

> **²⁰** Then Isaiah is so bold as to say,
>
>> "I have been found by those who did not seek me;
>> I have shown myself to those who did not ask for me."
>
> **²¹** But of Israel he says, "All day long I have held out my hands to a disobedient and contrary people." (10:19–21)

Drawing from Deuteronomy 32:21, Paul reminds the Jews of God's warning back in the nation's early days. Israel hadn't listened. They wanted to believe that God's blessings were reserved exclusively for them. So as the Gentiles are added in and given these blessings, Israel is indignant—jealous—that the Lord would share Israel's special privileges with those they see as "foolish" (idol worshiping) outsiders.

✤ According to Paul's quote from Isaiah in Romans 10:20, how did the Gentiles find the Lord?

_____

_____

_____

_____

✤ God's plan was never either-or (Israel or Gentiles) but always both-and. At a time when the church at Rome was made up mostly of believing Gentiles, what would Paul's Isaiah quote in 10:21 have communicated to both Jews and Gentiles?

_____

_____

_____

_____

3. A REMNANT (11:1–12)

Israel has rejected the Lord's Messiah, refusing to believe in him and in what he came to, but the Lord hasn't rejected them:

> ¹I ask, then, has God rejected his people? By no means! For I myself am an Israelite, a descendant of Abraham, a member of the tribe of Benjamin. ²God has not rejected his people whom he foreknew. Do you not know what the Scripture says of Elijah, how he appeals to God against Israel? ³"Lord, they have killed your prophets, they have demolished your altars, and I alone am left, and they seek my life." ⁴But what is God's reply to him? "I have kept for myself seven thousand men who have not bowed the knee to Baal." ⁵So too at the present time there is a remnant, chosen by grace. ⁶But if it is by grace, it is no longer on the basis of works; otherwise grace would no longer be grace. (11:1–6)

✧ Why would Paul's reminder of his Jewish background prove his point that God hasn't rejected Israel?

Paul recounts something that happened to Elijah the prophet back in a day when Israel was particularly unfaithful to God's covenant (you can read the exciting story in 1 Kings 19). Elijah demonstrated the Lord's power in a mighty way, only to have his life threatened by Israel's power-hungry leadership. Elijah ran away to hide from the threat, but the Lord met him there and called him to return to his people. Elijah complained that he was the only one left in Israel to uphold the Lord's honor, but the Lord told him, "I have kept for myself seven thousand men who have not bowed the knee to Baal." Baal was an idol, a false god, and at the time of Elijah, Israel had been participating in Baal worship. So God was saying to Elijah that from among all the apostate Israelites, he had set apart a very large number—too many to count—(which is what "seven thousand" represents) to save.

✧ In the midst of Israel's full-scale rejection of God, a select number—a remnant—will turn back. What word is applied repeatedly in 11:5–6 to this remnant?

Romans 10:1–11:36

✦ According to 11:6, what is the Elijah episode meant to illustrate?

The remnant of Israel continues to come to faith, but much of Israel has been lost:

> ⁷ What then? Israel failed to obtain what it was seeking. The elect obtained it, but the rest were hardened, ⁸ as it is written,
>
> > "God gave them a spirit of stupor,
> > > eyes that would not see
> > > and ears that would not hear,
> > down to this very day."
>
> ⁹ And David says,
>
> > "Let their table become a snare and a trap,
> > > a stumbling block and a retribution for them;
> > ¹⁰ let their eyes be darkened so that they cannot see,
> > > and bend their backs forever." (11:7–10)

✦ How do these quotes from the Old Testament remind you of what happened to Pharaoh in Egypt? Look back at the "Pharaoh's Heart" chart on pages 75–76 if you need a reminder.

Yes, much of Israel has been lost, but that's not the end of the story—for the Jews and for everyone. God has always had a plan for Israel:

> ¹¹ So I ask, did they stumble in order that they might fall? By no means! Rather, through their trespass salvation has come to the Gentiles, so as to make Israel jealous. ¹² Now if their trespass means riches for the world, and if their failure means riches for the Gentiles, how much more will their full inclusion mean! (11:11–12)

✦ What good does God plan to bring from Israel's rejection of Christ?

These riches are all the benefits that accompany salvation, seen in the golden chain of Romans 8:29–30. The "full inclusion" of the Jews is the remnant, those God has chosen to bring to saving faith.

4. FIRSTFRUITS AND GRAFTED BRANCHES (11:13–24)

For the first time in the letter, Paul writes directly to the Gentiles:

> ¹³ Now I am speaking to you Gentiles. Inasmuch then as I am an apostle to the Gentiles, I magnify my ministry ¹⁴ in order somehow to make my fellow Jews jealous, and thus save some of them. ¹⁵ For if their rejection means the reconciliation of the world, what will their acceptance mean but life from the dead? ¹⁶ If the dough offered as firstfruits is holy, so is the whole lump, and if the root is holy, so are the branches. (11:13–16)

✦ Paul had been set apart by God to preach the gospel to the Gentiles, and he seeks to steward his ministry well. What motivation for his Gentile ministry does he reveal here?

As we learned earlier, Israel's rejection of Christ opened the door for those of other nations to come in. This, in turn, makes the Jews jealous—they resent sharing God's blessings with non-Jews. If, as a result, the Jews turn and embrace the Savior, it's nothing short of the dead coming back to life.

- How does this plan and the way it unfolds over centuries enrich your knowledge of how God accomplishes his purposes?

The holy "dough offered as firstfruits" is a reference to Israel's annual harvest feast, which was established in Leviticus 23:17–21. The "firstfruits" and the "root" likely represent Israel's patriarchs Abraham, Isaac, and Jacob and the promises God made to them. Paul is saying that if the firstfruits and the root were set apart for God, so is the rest of Israel. But Paul isn't saying that *all* Jews will be saved. Rather, he's saying that God will be faithful to save a *remnant* of them. That's what Paul has in mind here. He wants the Gentile Christians in Rome to understand that Israel still has a vital place in God's plan:

> ¹⁷ But if some of the branches were broken off, and you, although a wild olive shoot, were grafted in among the others and now share in the nourishing root of the olive tree, ¹⁸ do not be arrogant toward the branches. If you are, remember it is not you who support the root, but the root that supports you. ¹⁹ Then you will say, "Branches were broken off so that I might be grafted in." ²⁰ That is true. They were broken off because of their unbelief, but you stand fast through faith. So do not become proud, but fear. ²¹ For if God did not spare the natural branches, neither will he spare you. ²² Note then the kindness and the severity of God: severity toward those who have fallen, but God's kindness to you, provided you continue in his kindness. Otherwise you too will be cut off. ²³ And even they, if they do not continue in their unbelief, will be grafted in, for God has the power to graft them in again. ²⁴ For if you were cut from what is by nature a wild olive tree, and grafted, contrary to nature, into a cultivated olive tree, how much more will these, the natural branches, be grafted back into their own olive tree. (11:17–24)

✦ What does Paul's warning to the Gentiles seem to indicate about what was happening among those in the Roman church?

✦ What does Paul tell the Gentiles to keep them humble?

5. MYSTERY MADE KNOWN (11:25–32)

Paul continues his efforts to keep the Gentiles humble:

> ²⁵ Lest you be wise in your own sight, I do not want you to be unaware of this mystery, brothers: a partial hardening has come upon Israel, until the fullness of the Gentiles has come in. ²⁶ And in this way all Israel will be saved, as it is written,
>
> > "The Deliverer will come from Zion,
> > he will banish ungodliness from Jacob";
> > ²⁷ "and this will be my covenant with them
> > when I take away their sins."
>
> ²⁸ As regards the gospel, they are enemies for your sake. But as regards election, they are beloved for the sake of their forefathers. ²⁹ For the gifts and the calling of God are irrevocable. ³⁰ For just as you were at one time disobedient to God but now have received mercy because of their disobedience, ³¹ so they too have now been disobedient in order that by the mercy shown to you they also may now receive mercy. ³² For God has consigned all to disobedience, that he may have mercy on all. (11:25–32)

Romans 10:1–11:36

✦ The "mystery" isn't a perplexing puzzle of some sort. It's about something that was hidden but is now revealed. What is uncovered in verse 25?

It's important to note that when Paul writes that "all Israel will be saved" (11:26), he is speaking not about *ethnic* Israel but about *spiritual* Israel. In other words, all the Jews whom God has chosen to save will be saved. They are "enemies" of the gospel at present because that's part of God's plan for gathering in believers from other nations.

✦ Paul has written already about Israel being made jealous through God's extending his grace to Gentiles. Where do you get a glimpse of that jealousy in this passage?

6. A FITTING CONCLUSION (11:33–36)

The final verses of Romans 11 are a doxology, a pouring out of praise. This praise here in the letter shows us that Paul has finished setting out the details of God's magnificent plan for salvation. And praise is absolutely fitting in light of all we've learned in these eleven chapters:

> ³³ Oh, the depth of the riches and wisdom and knowledge of God! How unsearchable are his judgments and how inscrutable his ways!
> ³⁴ "For who has known the mind of the Lord,
>   or who has been his counselor?"
> ³⁵ "Or who has given a gift to him
>   that he might be repaid?"
> ³⁶ For from him and through him and to him are all things. To him be glory forever. Amen. (11:33–36)

- What do you think Paul means when he writes that God's ways are "unsearchable" and "inscrutable"?

- How would you answer the questions Paul asks in 11:34–35, words he borrows from Isaiah 40:13?

- Write a summary of Romans 11:36 in your own words.

> *"The reason why people don't come to God is not because God fails to invite them, nor is it a logical conclusion from the doctrine of predestination, but it is rooted in disobedience and obstinacy. . . . Anyone can be saved if he wants to be saved, but therein lies the problem. No one wants to be saved, unless God sovereignly plants a desire in the rebellious heart to come to him."*[23]

LET'S TALK

1. Paul grieved for his Jewish kinsmen because they had "a zeal for God, but not according to knowledge" (10:2). When we see or experience energetic passion for ministry endeavors, how can we know whether it's genuine? What sort of motives should we be aware of in discerning the difference?

2. God's word proclaimed is God's primary instrument for working salvation into unsaved hearts. As preachers preach the gospel, and as we tell the good news to our lost friends and neighbors, the Spirit is at work. Can you describe a time when you realized that God had been working "behind the scenes" as you shared the gospel?

3. Paul warned the Gentile believers against arrogance, believing their embrace of the gospel made them superior to the Jews who were stuck in the old-covenant system. What spiritual privileges have you received that tempt you to feel superior to others? Consider things like growing up in a Christian home, attending seminary, belonging to a certain denomination, or sitting under the preaching of a "celebrity" pastor.

WEEK 9

BE WHAT YOU ARE

ROMANS 12:1–15:13

We've learned so much! For the past eight weeks, we've been immersed in the gospel, finding out how God justifies sinners and discovering what it means to be united to Christ by faith. So now what? How do these great realities impact our day-to-day lives? That's what these next chapters in Romans teach us, how to apply these great doctrines of salvation. Here we see, first and foremost, what our union with Christ means for our relationship with God now, in the present. Life in Christ impacts everything about us. The apostle is going to show us how to thrive in our relationships with our brothers and sisters in Christ and how to reflect Christ to the unbelievers we encounter in everyday life. Overall, these chapters paint a comprehensive picture of holy living in service to the one who has given us everything, the Lord Jesus Christ.

1. LIVING SACRIFICES (12:1–2)

All Paul's instructions in this section, which covers 12:1–15:13, flow from how he begins here:

> ¹ I appeal to you therefore, brothers, by the mercies of God, to present your bodies as a living sacrifice, holy and acceptable to God, which is your spiritual worship. ² Do not be conformed to this world, but be transformed by the renewal of your mind, that by testing you may discern what is the will of God, what is good and acceptable and perfect. (12:1–2)

✟ In the covenant of the Old Testament, God's people offered sacrifices of grain and animals. In the new covenant established in Christ's blood, people offer themselves. How does Paul define this offering in verse 1?

✟ Verse 2 contains a positive command and a negative one. They are both necessary and, in fact, work together to grow us in holiness. On a practical level, how do we keep from being conformed to worldly ways and at the same time renew our minds?

> *"When Paul encourages us to prove that God's will is a pleasing will, he obviously means pleasing to us. That is, if we determine to walk in God's way, refusing to be conformed to the world and being transformed instead by the renewing of our minds, we will not have to fear that at the end of our lives we will look back and be dissatisfied or bitter, judging our lives to have been an utter waste. On the contrary, we will look back and conclude that our lives were well lived and be satisfied with them."*[24]

2. ALL FOR ONE, AND ONE FOR ALL (12:3-21)

We've picked up on some possible tensions in the Roman church—Jews and Gentile converts looking down on one another for both past and present differences in their spiritual lives. So for them, and for all of us in the church today, Paul places a strong emphasis on unity:

> ³ For by the grace given to me I say to everyone among you not to think of himself more highly than he ought to think, but to think with sober judgment, each according to the measure of faith that God has assigned. ⁴ For as in one body we have many members, and the members do not all have the same function, ⁵ so we, though many, are one body in Christ, and individually members one of another. ⁶ Having gifts that differ according to the grace given to us, let us use them: if prophecy, in proportion to our faith; ⁷ if service, in our serving; the one who teaches, in his teaching; ⁸ the one who exhorts, in his exhortation; the one who contributes, in generosity; the one who leads, with zeal; the one who does acts of mercy, with cheerfulness. (12:3–8)

✦ Why do you think humility is an important component of unity among believers?

✦ Paul instructs Christians in no uncertain terms to put their spiritual gifts to use. How does his metaphor of a body demonstrate how these gifts are meant to function?

Spiritual Gifts in Romans 12:6-8	
Gift	Using the Gift
Prophesying (v. 6)	Proclaiming God's revelation
Serving (v. 7)	Helping those in need
Teaching (v. 7)	Instructing others in God's word and ways
Exhorting (v. 8)	Encouraging, comforting, and warning
Contributing (v. 8)	Giving freely of personal resources
Leading (v. 8)	Presiding over others for their well-being, as elders do

He also lists distinctive character qualities that mark Christians as belonging to Christ:

> [9] Let love be genuine. Abhor what is evil; hold fast to what is good. [10] Love one another with brotherly affection. Outdo one another in showing honor. [11] Do not be slothful in zeal, be fervent in spirit, serve the Lord. [12] Rejoice in hope, be patient in tribulation, be constant in prayer. [13] Contribute to the needs of the saints and seek to show hospitality.
>
> [14] Bless those who persecute you; bless and do not curse them. [15] Rejoice with those who rejoice, weep with those who weep. [16] Live in harmony with one

Romans 12:1–15:13

another. Do not be haughty, but associate with the lowly. Never be wise in your own sight. ¹⁷ Repay no one evil for evil, but give thought to do what is honorable in the sight of all. ¹⁸ If possible, so far as it depends on you, live peaceably with all. ¹⁹ Beloved, never avenge yourselves, but leave it to the wrath of God, for it is written, "Vengeance is mine, I will repay, says the Lord." ²⁰ To the contrary, "if your enemy is hungry, feed him; if he is thirsty, give him something to drink; for by so doing you will heap burning coals on his head." ²¹ Do not be overcome by evil, but overcome evil with good. (12:9–21)

✤ What does it mean to "abhor" evil?

✤ Paul showcases a holy enthusiasm within the church. Why do you think this is important?

✤ Disagreements, misunderstandings, and sins mar human relationships, even within the church. Paul cites Jesus as well as the Old Testament to instruct us in how to handle these relational breaches. Note what you see in 12:18–21 about the Christ-honoring way to deal with relational breaches.

3. SERVING ALL GOD'S SERVANTS (13:1–14)

Offering ourselves as living sacrifices to God includes not only how we treat our brothers and sisters in Christ but also how we conduct ourselves in society:

> ¹Let every person be subject to the governing authorities. For there is no authority except from God, and those that exist have been instituted by God. ²Therefore whoever resists the authorities resists what God has appointed, and those who resist will incur judgment. ³For rulers are not a terror to good conduct, but to bad. Would you have no fear of the one who is in authority? Then do what is good, and you will receive his approval, ⁴for he is God's servant for your good. But if you do wrong, be afraid, for he does not bear the sword in vain. For he is the servant of God, an avenger who carries out God's wrath on the wrongdoer. ⁵Therefore one must be in subjection, not only to avoid God's wrath but also for the sake of conscience. ⁶For because of this you also pay taxes, for the authorities are ministers of God, attending to this very thing. ⁷Pay to all what is owed to them: taxes to whom taxes are owed, revenue to whom revenue is owed, respect to whom respect is owed, honor to whom honor is owed. (13:1–7)

✦ What spiritual reason does Paul give in verses 1–2 for why we must submit to our government?

✦ In what way are governing authorities God's servants?

✦ What might tempt you to compromise paying money, respect, or honor as Paul instructs in 13:7?

As we learned earlier in our study, we don't earn favor with God by keeping his law, but that doesn't free us from the obligation to obey it. We keep it now *not* to earn his favor but because we already have it. Paul describes what Christian law-keeping looks like:

> ⁸ Owe no one anything, except to love each other, for the one who loves another has fulfilled the law. ⁹ For the commandments, "You shall not commit adultery, You shall not murder, You shall not steal, You shall not covet," and any other commandment, are summed up in this word: "You shall love your neighbor as yourself." ¹⁰ Love does no wrong to a neighbor; therefore love is the fulfilling of the law. (13:8–10)

✦ What has always been the overarching purpose for all the various commandments in God's law?

Spiritual sluggishness must be cast off because we don't know when Christ will return to take us home to heaven for eternity:

> ¹¹ Besides this you know the time, that the hour has come for you to wake from sleep. For salvation is nearer to us now than when we first believed. ¹² The night is far gone; the day is at hand. So then let us cast off the works of darkness and put on the armor of light. ¹³ Let us walk properly as in the daytime, not in orgies and drunkenness, not in sexual immorality and sensuality, not in quarreling

and jealousy. ¹⁴ But put on the Lord Jesus Christ, and make no provision for the flesh, to gratify its desires. (13:11–14)

✢ Christ could return at any time, and when he does, we want to be ready. The "night" is everything that's wrapped up with worldly sinfulness, and we are to cast off the attitudes and activities that tempt us as we'd toss away filthy clothes. How does 13:13–14 show us how to cast off dark works and put on "the armor of light" (13:12)?

Paul's words are a call "for us to wear Jesus wherever we go ... so that we are regularly modeling ... his Godward life of a holy heart, a holy mind, and a submissive will to God the Father."²⁵

4. DON'T JUDGE! (14:1-14)

"You do you" is contemporary jargon for acceptance to those whose choices differ from ours. Paul is advocating for something similar as he continues to show us how Christian love is lived out:

> ¹ As for the one who is weak in faith, welcome him, but not to quarrel over opinions. ² One person believes he may eat anything, while the weak person eats only vegetables. ³ Let not the one who eats despise the one who abstains, and let not the one who abstains pass judgment on the one who eats, for God has welcomed him. ⁴ Who are you to pass judgment on the servant of another? It is before his own master that he stands or falls. And he will be upheld, for the Lord is able to make him stand. (14:1–4)

Specifically in mind here are those gray areas, things in life that aren't spelled out as black or white in Scripture. Theologians refer to such things as "secondary matters." As we dig into what Paul is saying here, let's remember what was going on in the church at Rome. The church was made up of Gentile Christians and Jews who had embraced Christ as Lord, but deeply entrenched customs and practices from their respective backgrounds hindered their fellowship. The Jews continued to observe some of the food laws that were required under the Old Testament covenant—not as a means of being saved but because, even though they were free from those laws, their consciences were bothered by eating those foods. Paul refers to them as "weak in faith."

✦ How does Paul urge each side to respond to the other side?

- The weak in faith:

- Those who eat freely:

✦ What is the basis for Paul's instructions to both sides?

Paul gives the same guidance concerning the observance of Old Testament religious holidays:

> ⁵One person esteems one day as better than another, while another esteems all days alike. Each one should be fully convinced in his own mind. ⁶The one who observes the day, observes it in honor of the Lord. The one who eats, eats in honor of the Lord, since he gives thanks to God, while the one who abstains, abstains in honor of the Lord and gives thanks to God. ⁷For none of us lives to himself, and none of us dies to himself. ⁸For if we live, we live to the Lord, and if we die, we die to the Lord. So then, whether we live or whether we die,

we are the Lord's. ⁹ For to this end Christ died and lived again, that he might be Lord both of the dead and of the living.

¹⁰ Why do you pass judgment on your brother? Or you, why do you despise your brother? For we will all stand before the judgment seat of God; ¹¹ for it is written,

> "As I live, says the Lord, every knee shall bow to me,
> and every tongue shall confess to God."

¹² So then each of us will give an account of himself to God. (14:5–12)

Some believe that the "day" in 14:5 is the Sabbath, which God commanded his people to set apart for rest and worship. Keeping the Sabbath is one of the Ten Commandments, the moral law, which, unlike the old-covenant civil and ceremonial laws, was not abolished in Christ. For that reason, it's more likely that Paul has in mind the observance of old-covenant ceremonies and feasts, which were civil and ceremonial. This view also ties in best with what Paul's been saying about certain foods.

✦ What is Paul's primary point in 14:5–12?

....

....

....

....

And now Paul gets to the heart of his lesson here:

> ¹³ Therefore let us not pass judgment on one another any longer, but rather decide never to put a stumbling block or hindrance in the way of a brother. ¹⁴ I know and am persuaded in the Lord Jesus that nothing is unclean in itself, but it is unclean for anyone who thinks it unclean. ¹⁵ For if your brother is grieved by what you eat, you are no longer walking in love. By what you eat, do not destroy the one for whom Christ died. ¹⁶ So do not let what you regard as good be spoken of as evil. ¹⁷ For the kingdom of God is not a matter of eating and drinking but of righteousness and peace and joy in the Holy Spirit. ¹⁸ Whoever thus serves Christ is acceptable to God and approved by men. ¹⁹ So then let us pursue what makes for peace and for mutual upbuilding. (14:13–19)

Romans 12:1–15:13

✦ How can those whose conscience allows them to enjoy all food demonstrate love to those whose conscience isn't free?

He has a clear message for both—those whose consciences are free and those whose consciences are bothered:

> [20] Do not, for the sake of food, destroy the work of God. Everything is indeed clean, but it is wrong for anyone to make another stumble by what he eats. It is good not to eat meat or drink wine or do anything that causes your brother to stumble. The faith that you have, keep between yourself and God. Blessed is the one who has no reason to pass judgment on himself for what he approves. But whoever has doubts is condemned if he eats, because the eating is not from faith. For whatever does not proceed from faith is sin. (14:20–23)

✦ According to 14:23, what is the godly way to respond to a bothered conscience?

5. WHAT LOVE LOOKS LIKE (15:1-13)

When it comes to handling these matters, here's our greatest motivation:

> [1] We who are strong have an obligation to bear with the failings of the weak, and not to please ourselves. [2] Let each of us please his neighbor for his good, to build him up. [3] For Christ did not please himself, but as it is written, "The reproaches of those who reproached you fell on me." [4] For whatever was written in former days was written for our instruction, that through endurance and through the encouragement of the Scriptures we might have hope. [5] May

the God of endurance and encouragement grant you to live in such harmony with one another, in accord with Christ Jesus, ⁶ that together you may with one voice glorify the God and Father of our Lord Jesus Christ. ⁷ Therefore welcome one another as Christ has welcomed you, for the glory of God. (15:1–7)

✦ If our conscience is free to enjoy something, how can we demonstrate Christlike love to those who don't feel free?

✦ What is the overarching reason that Jews and Gentiles—all believers—should strive for unity, even when (maybe especially when) it necessitates personal sacrifice?

Loving sacrificially is hard, even toward those for whom we feel lots of personal affection. We need some motivation to persevere, and as Paul ends this exhortation, he gives us just what we need:

> ⁸ For I tell you that Christ became a servant to the circumcised to show God's truthfulness, in order to confirm the promises given to the patriarchs, ⁹ and in order that the Gentiles might glorify God for his mercy. As it is written,
>
> > "Therefore I will praise you among the Gentiles,
> >   and sing to your name."
>
> ¹⁰ And again it is said,
>
> > "Rejoice, O Gentiles, with his people."

¹¹ And again,

> "Praise the Lord, all you Gentiles,
>   and let all the peoples extol him."

¹² And again Isaiah says,

> "The root of Jesse will come,
>   even he who arises to rule the Gentiles;
> in him will the Gentiles hope."

¹³ May the God of hope fill you with all joy and peace in believing, so that by the power of the Holy Spirit you may abound in hope. (15:8–13)

LET'S TALK

1. Talk about how Romans 12:1–2 is the necessary foundation for living the way Paul outlines for us in these chapters.

2. We read in 13:14, "Put on the Lord Jesus Christ, and make no provision for the flesh, to gratify its desires." Talk about what "making no provision" will require you to do.

3. Paul instructs, "If your brother is grieved by what you eat, you are no longer walking in love. By what you eat, do not destroy the one for whom Christ died" (14:15). Is there something you need to give up for the sake of conscience, whether your own or someone else's? Share why letting it go is difficult.

WEEK 10

A PORTRAIT OF FAITHFULNESS

ROMANS 15:14–16:27

We get many clues about Paul's life and ministry as he begins to wrap up the letter. Here we find some personal details about the apostle and about his mission and the specific people he cares about. Studying Romans is like drinking from a spiritual firehose, so by now, it's hard to take in more—especially a portion that seems so far removed from our life today and focuses on people we've never heard of. If you're feeling that way, maybe these words will help you persevere through this last section: "Sadly, this is a section that many could see as miscellaneous or minor. However, ... we should not think this. To the contrary, what we have here gives us many useful insights into Paul's pastoral character, commission, and concerns. Because of this, we should take special heed to it."[26] I hope you feel inspired as we begin our final lesson!

1. A FAITHFUL PASTOR (15:14–21)

As Paul begins to wrap up the letter, he reflects on his ministry:

> [14] I myself am satisfied about you, my brothers, that you yourselves are full of goodness, filled with all knowledge and able to instruct one another. [15] But on some points I have written to you very boldly by way of reminder, because of the grace given me by God [16] to be a minister of Christ Jesus to the Gentiles in the priestly service of the gospel of God, so that the offering of the Gentiles may be acceptable, sanctified by the Holy Spirit. [17] In Christ Jesus, then, I have reason to be proud of my work for God. [18] For I will not venture to speak of anything except what Christ has accomplished through me to bring the Gentiles

to obedience—by word and deed, ¹⁹ by the power of signs and wonders, by the power of the Spirit of God—so that from Jerusalem and all the way around to Illyricum I have fulfilled the ministry of the gospel of Christ; ²⁰ and thus I make it my ambition to preach the gospel, not where Christ has already been named, lest I build on someone else's foundation, ²¹ but as it is written,

> "Those who have never been told of him will see,
>   and those who have never heard will understand." (15:14–21)

✦ How does Paul encourage the believers in the church at Rome?

In the Old Testament, the priests were the ones who presented the people's sacrifices and offerings to God in the tabernacle and, later, in the temple. Paul sees his ministry in a similar light, but the offering he brings to God is the people themselves, the Gentiles who come to faith through his preaching.

✦ To what does Paul attribute the success of his ministry?

Paul strategized specific places to take the gospel message, being careful to focus his efforts on unreached areas and to bypass places where others were already ministering. In this way, he was actually fulfilling a particular prophecy found in Isaiah 52:15, which Paul quotes here in 15:21.

2. A FAITHFUL PLANNER (15:22–29)

As Paul shares his plans, we get an inside look into his life and longings:

Romans 15:14–16:27

> ²²This is the reason why I have so often been hindered from coming to you. ²³But now, since I no longer have any room for work in these regions, and since I have longed for many years to come to you, ²⁴I hope to see you in passing as I go to Spain, and to be helped on my journey there by you, once I have enjoyed your company for a while. ²⁵At present, however, I am going to Jerusalem bringing aid to the saints. ²⁶For Macedonia and Achaia have been pleased to make some contribution for the poor among the saints at Jerusalem. ²⁷For they were pleased to do it, and indeed they owe it to them. For if the Gentiles have come to share in their spiritual blessings, they ought also to be of service to them in material blessings. ²⁸When therefore I have completed this and have delivered to them what has been collected, I will leave for Spain by way of you. ²⁹I know that when I come to you I will come in the fullness of the blessing of Christ. (15:22–29)

✝ Paul has yet to visit the believers in Rome. What is the reason for the hindrance he alludes to in verse 22? (Hint: look back at verses 18–21.)

✝ What do we learn in this passage about the way in which the body of Christ thrives?

3. PRAYER PARTNERS (15:30–33)

Paul opens up about his personal concerns:

> ³⁰I appeal to you, brothers, by our Lord Jesus Christ and by the love of the Spirit, to strive together with me in your prayers to God on my behalf, that I may be delivered from the unbelievers in Judea, and that my service for Jerusalem may be acceptable to the saints, so that by God's will I may come to you with joy and be refreshed in your company. May the God of peace be with you all. Amen. (15:30–33)

Paul has two prayer requests: (1) that he won't be held up by unbelieving Jews who were persecuting Christians (as Paul himself had done before his conversion), and (2) that the offering he has orchestrated for the Jerusalem church would be accepted.

✣ Paul's concern about the Jerusalem church is that troublemakers had spread false reports about him and that these reports had reached Jerusalem and poisoned the minds of the believers there. According to Acts 21:17, how was this prayer answered?

Romans 15:33 is another benediction—a blessing Paul holds out to the recipients of his letter. Salvation in Christ brings us peace with God and peace with one another, and the hope here is that we will be characterized by it.

> *May the God of peace be with you all.*
> *Amen. (Romans 15:33)*

4. THE BOND OF BELIEVERS (16:1–16)

As the letter draws to a close, Paul sends greetings to dear friends and ministry partners at the church in Rome:

> ¹ I commend to you our sister Phoebe, a servant of the church at Cenchreae, ² that you may welcome her in the Lord in a way worthy of the saints, and help her in whatever she may need from you, for she has been a patron of many and of myself as well.
> ³ Greet Prisca and Aquila, my fellow workers in Christ Jesus, ⁴ who risked their necks for my life, to whom not only I give thanks but all the churches of the Gentiles give thanks as well. ⁵ Greet also the church in their house. Greet my beloved Epaenetus, who was the first convert to Christ in Asia. ⁶ Greet Mary, who has worked hard for you. ⁷ Greet Andronicus and Junia, my kinsmen and

my fellow prisoners. They are well known to the apostles, and they were in Christ before me. ⁸ Greet Ampliatus, my beloved in the Lord. ⁹ Greet Urbanus, our fellow worker in Christ, and my beloved Stachys. ¹⁰ Greet Apelles, who is approved in Christ. Greet those who belong to the family of Aristobulus. ¹¹ Greet my kinsman Herodion. Greet those in the Lord who belong to the family of Narcissus. ¹² Greet those workers in the Lord, Tryphaena and Tryphosa. Greet the beloved Persis, who has worked hard in the Lord. ¹³ Greet Rufus, chosen in the Lord; also his mother, who has been a mother to me as well. ¹⁴ Greet Asyncritus, Phlegon, Hermes, Patrobas, Hermas, and the brothers who are with them. ¹⁵ Greet Philologus, Julia, Nereus and his sister, and Olympas, and all the saints who are with them. ¹⁶ Greet one another with a holy kiss. All the churches of Christ greet you. (16:1–16)

Phoebe

"It was not very safe for a woman to travel alone in the ancient world, so Phoebe probably had people with her. But it is Phoebe mentioned and not these other persons—not even a husband—so we are probably right to suppose that she was single and a prominent woman. She must have been wealthy too, because it took money to travel."²⁷

Paul first commends Phoebe, and from his wording in verse 2, it's likely that she is the one who carried this letter on Paul's behalf to Rome. Paul identifies Phoebe as a "servant" of the church. Some think that the word "servant" Paul uses here indicates that Phoebe held the official role of deaconess in the early church. That's all we know about her—that she served the church faithfully.

If you've read the book of Acts and Paul's other epistles, you'll recognize some of the names in these greetings.

✚ What do we learn about Prisca (Priscilla) and Aquila in 16:4–5? (To get a sense of the couple's history with Paul, you'll find it in Acts 18:1–28.)

> "God's ways are not our ways. Therefore, be prepared for new things and for unexpected circumstances. Although the task of taking the gospel to the lost remains unchanged, God will probably accomplish your part of it in ways you do not anticipate."[28]

✦ On this list we see Gentiles and Jewish converts (Paul's kinsmen), rich and poor, men and women. What stands out to you in these greetings about the Christians in Rome and about Paul himself?

5. A FINAL WARNING (16:17–20)

We typically know how to guard ourselves against worldly influences, people and situations that tempt us to compromise our faithfulness to Christ. Recognizing bad influences within Christian circles is a lot harder and requires discernment. This is the very issue Paul chooses for his last bit of instruction to the believers in Rome:

> [17] I appeal to you, brothers, to watch out for those who cause divisions and create obstacles contrary to the doctrine that you have been taught; avoid them. [18] For such persons do not serve our Lord Christ, but their own appetites, and by smooth talk and flattery they deceive the hearts of the naive. [19] For your obedience is known to all, so that I rejoice over you, but I want you to be wise as to what is good and innocent as to what is evil. [20] The God of peace will soon crush Satan under your feet. The grace of our Lord Jesus Christ be with you. (16:17–20)

✦ What does Paul reveal about false teachers in these verses that can help us be discerning?

Romans 15:14–16:27

✤ We are told in verse 17 that false teachers are to be avoided. Why do you think Paul urges such a radical approach?

✤ Paul links false teaching to Satan—a powerful enemy—yet his words in 16:20 point back to Christ's victory over Satan on the cross and give us hope to persevere. How does Genesis 3:14–15 show us this connection?

> "How did Paul come to know and actually love so many Christians? How did he remember them all? Chiefly because he was thinking about them rather than about himself."[29]

6. GLORY FOREVERMORE (16:21-27)

Paul sends final greetings, this time from those who are ministering alongside him, and then he ends with a glorious doxology, an expression of praise to God, that basically summarizes all he has written in the letter about the gospel:

²¹ Timothy, my fellow worker, greets you; so do Lucius and Jason and Sosipater, my kinsmen.

²² I Tertius, who wrote this letter, greet you in the Lord.

²³ Gaius, who is host to me and to the whole church, greets you. Erastus, the city treasurer, and our brother Quartus, greet you.

²⁵ Now to him who is able to strengthen you according to my gospel and the preaching of Jesus Christ, according to the revelation of the mystery that was kept secret for long ages ²⁶ but has now been disclosed and through the prophetic writings has been made known to all nations, according to the command of the eternal God, to bring about the obedience of faith—²⁷ to the only wise God be glory forevermore through Jesus Christ! Amen. (16:21–27)

From Paul's other letters, especially those he wrote directly to Timothy, we know that Timothy was like a son to Paul. He loved him dearly. Included in these final greetings is a man named Tertius, who served as Paul's secretary. Paul dictated this letter to Tertius, who was careful to relay faithfully all Paul said.

✦ Make a list of God's attributes that are praised in Paul's closing doxology.

LET'S TALK

1. Discuss what we can we learn from Paul's lengthy greetings about how life is meant to be lived with our brothers and sisters in Christ and how our churches can grow in love for one another.

2. How can we learn to detect unbiblical teaching about God and the gospel? It lurks in books, podcasts, social media, and, as Paul reveals, even in some of our very own churches. Discuss where you've encountered unbiblical teaching and what you have done—or will do—to avoid it.

3. As we come to the end of Romans, note what you've learned or what's affected you most about—

• the character of God:

- the gospel of salvation through Jesus Christ:

- the path of discipleship:

HELPFUL RESOURCES FOR STUDYING ROMANS

Boice, James Montgomery. *Romans: An Expositional Commentary*. 4 vols. Grand Rapids, MI: Baker, 1991.

Guthrie, Nancy, host. "Michael Kruger on Romans 1–7." *Help Me Teach the Bible* podcast, December 15, 2016. https://www.thegospelcoalition.org.

Guthrie, Nancy, host. "Michael Kruger on Romans 8–16." *Help Me Teach the Bible* podcast, December 29, 2016. https://www.thegospelcoalition.org.

Naselli, Andrew David. *Romans: A Concise Guide to the Greatest Letter Ever Written*. Wheaton, IL: Crossway, 2022.

Ventura, Rob. *Expository Outlines and Observations on Romans: Hints and Helps for Preachers and Teachers*. Ross-shire, UK: Mentor, 2023.

NOTES

1. "Rome in the Time of Paul" map from page 2153 of the ESV® Study Bible (The Holy Bible, English Standard Version®), © 2008 by Crossway, a publishing ministry of Good News Publishers. Used by permission. All rights reserved.
2. John Piper, "The Author of the Greatest Letter Ever Written" (sermon, Bethlehem Baptist Church, Minneapolis, MN, April 26, 1998), https://www.desiringgod.org/.
3. Rob Ventura, *Expository Outlines and Observations on Romans: Hints and Helps for Preachers and Teachers* (Ross-shire, UK: Mentor, 2023), 26.
4. Ventura, *Expository Outlines*, 29.
5. James Montgomery Boice, *Romans: An Expository Commentary* (Grand Rapids, MI: Baker, 1991), 1:24.
6. John H. Gerstner, cited in Boice, *Romans*, 1:186.
7. ESV Study Bible (Wheaton, IL: Crossway, 2008), note on Romans 1:23.
8. Boice, *Romans*, 1:14.
9. Adapted from Stephen Nichols, "The Doctrine of Imputation," Ligonier, April 16, 2016, https://www.ligonier.org/.
10. Andrew D. Naselli, *Romans: A Concise Guide to the Greatest Letter Ever Written* (Wheaton, IL: Crossway, 2022), 45.
11. ESV Study Bible, note on Romans 2:25.
12. Boice, *Romans*, 1:208.
13. I am grateful to Rob Ventura for this helpful summary of the Jewish objection as "equal footing."
14. Boice, *Romans*, 1:359.
15. ESV Study Bible, note on Romans 5:14.
16. Boice, *Romans*, 2:598
17. D.M. Lloyd-Jones, *Romans: An Exposition of Chapter 5, Assurance* (Grand Rapids, MI: Zondervan, 1972), 356.
18. Boice, *Romans*, 2:638.

19. *Merriam-Webster*, s.v. "slavery (*n.*)," accessed April 10, 2024, www.merriam-webster.com.
20. Ventura, *Expository Outlines*, 210 emphasis added.
21. Ventura, *Expository Outlines*, 214.
22. Boice, *Romans*, 2:896.
23. R. C. Sproul, cited in Ventura, *Expository Outlines*, 292.
24. Boice, *Romans*, 4:1558–59.
25. Ventura, *Expository Outlines*, 360.
26. Ventura, *Expository Outlines*, 392.
27. Boice, *Romans*, 4:1913.
28. Boice, *Romans*, 4:1874.
29. Boice, *Romans*, 4:1925.

Flourish Bible Study Series

Judges	*Romans*
Esther	*Ephesians*
Job	*Philippians*
Ecclesiastes	*Colossians*
Jonah	*James*
Habakkuk	*1–2 Peter*
Luke	

For more information, visit **crossway.org**.